*To My Bride*

# CONTENTS

PREFACE . . . . . . . . . . . . . . . . . . . . . . . . . . . . . . . . . . . . . . . . . . . . . .VII

1. Our Prudery: An Introduction . . . . . . . . . . . . . . . . . . . . . . . . . . . . 1

2. Why We've Forgotten: Equality v. Nature . . . . . . . . . . . . . . . . . . . 7

3. How to Proceed: Past Acceptance...and Onward to Action . . . . . . . 18

4. What We've Forgotten: Nature's Stubborn Hard Facts . . . . . . . . . . . 21

5. What We've Forgotten: Nature's Stubborn Hopeful Facts . . . . . . . . . 50

6. How to Proceed: Dancing with Nature . . . . . . . . . . . . . . . . . . . . . . . 68

7. But Why Get Hitched? . . . . . . . . . . . . . . . . . . . . . . . . . . . . . . . . . . . 104

But the friendship of husband and wife seems to exist by nature, for men and women are naturally more inclined to live in pairs than in cities.

-Aristotle, *Nicomachean Ethics,* (c. 350 B.C.).


Dear, but let us type them now
In our own lives, and this proud watchword rest
Of equal; seeing either sex alone
Is half itself, and in true marriage lies
Nor equal, nor unequal:  each fulfills
Defect in each, and always thought in thought,
Purpose in purpose, will in will, they grow,
The single pure and perfect animal,
The two-celled heart beating, with one full stroke,
Life.

-Alfred Tennyson, *The Princess* (1847).

# PREFACE

**What This Book Is About** Breeder scum ♡

The majority of women and men want not only to have sex, but also to form lasting sexual relationships, maybe even get married, maybe even for life. But many are having a hard time getting there. In the past few decades, the marriage rate has declined dramatically, especially in the United States. While much of this change reflects *disinterest*, in many, many cases, it reflects *disappointment*. According to a recent Gallup poll, among the millions who had never married, 78% said they still would like to get hitched someday. Many are depressed. Some are angry.

The claim of this book is that this widespread disappointment arises in large part from an epidemic of *amnesia*. In so many ways, men and women have forgotten how to attract each other. Our ancestors knew how. But we don't.

In particular, our ancestors appreciated certain stubborn facts of life. They knew better what guys liked, what women wanted. Appreciation for these facts once formed an essential part of *common sense*.

But for reasons peculiar to our times, these facts have become obscure, even forgotten. The sexes are increasingly foreign to one another, and even to themselves. Alienation, perhaps, is the most precise term.

This amnesia is especially problematic in our times. When marriages were expected, if not arranged, the know-how was not very important. The young woman and the young man just needed to show up. But nowadays, aspiring spouses often have to figure it out on their own. The marriage-minded of today need the old common sense so much more that our ancestors did, but ironically, they often have so much less of it.

The somewhat immodest aim of this book is to refresh our recollection, that is, to rejuvenate the old common sense about what attracts men and women to each other as marriage partners. In the following chapters, I will sketch why we've forgotten, what we've forgotten, and how recovering that common sense can be so helpful in pursuing marriage.

### What This Book Is Not About

Because this book is about common sense, I do not provide any *secrets* in the manner of the so-called "relationship experts." This book is more a compilation of old wives' tales. "Old wives' tale" is usually a term of derision, but it shouldn't be. If there's anything old wives know better than anyone, is how to become an old wife—that is, how to get and stay married. We should listen to the old wives (and old husbands) if we want to join their increasingly exclusive club.

Indeed, this book involves very little *expertise*, whether scientific or otherwise. The evidence relied on here is, for the most part, readily and easily available. The average reader has already seen a lifetime of the relevant data. But many of us just can't see the obvious. To use a great old expression, the facts are as plain (but equally unseen) as the noses on our faces.

I'm a college professor. My academic expertise, such as it is, will be useful mainly in explaining the cause of this hyperopia (blindness to the things close by). I will contend that the answer to our romantic woes, strangely enough, can be found first by a brief look at a very unromantic subject: political philosophy. But for the most part, I will be simply collecting and restating what *can* and *should* be obvious.

Furthermore, this book treats only a *part* of the subject of mutual attraction: the stubborn bodily hardwiring that inclines so many women and men to desire an enduring domestic relationship with each other. So the book does not treat the higher aspects of attraction and mating—whether communicative, moral, religious, spiritual, or otherwise. Smarter people have already written many books on these more important matters.[1]

Similarly, this book does not treat all *relationships*. Because it concerns the sexes' mutual alienation, this book involves a problem peculiar to relations between men and women. Thus, the discussion will not cover same-sex relationships or any other bond that does not involve the obstacles peculiar to the domestic union of male and female.

For like reasons, this book is not about the many modern cultural and political disputes as to how marriage ought to be defined, regulated, etc. It doesn't, for instance, concern whether couples should get the "piece of paper" by civil marriage, or the many other related questions.

Finally, this book does not aim to persuade anyone that getting married is worthwhile. While I am married, and think it's a very good way of life, I doubt I could persuade anyone who disagrees.

To tell the truth, like all great enterprises, marriage involves guaranteed sacrifices but only uncertain joys. I think it's worth it. But many understandably conclude otherwise.

Instead of pleading the cause of marriage, I begin simply with the naked fact that even today, despite all the distrust and disappointment, many men and women, whether wisely or foolishly, seem incurably convinced that marriage is a good thing to pursue, but find the pursuit difficult, if not daunting. Whether you are such a person, or count such persons among your loved ones, I hope you will find my efforts here informative, entertaining, and above all, encouraging.

---

1  For some of these smarter people and their writings, see this fine anthology: Amy A. Kass and Leon R. Kass, eds., *Wing to Wing, Oar to Oar: Readings on Courting and Marrying* (Notre Dame, IN: University of Notre Dame Press, 2000).

# CHAPTER ONE

## OUR PRUDERY: AN INTRODUCTION

C andor is the pride of our age. We tell it like it is. We keep it real.

If candor is our crown, candor about sex is the jewel in the crown.

Indeed, for well over a century, we have talked incessantly about sex, tossed off all sorts of veils, and laughed off all kinds of taboos. Compared with the average Victorian, we are *much* more familiar with the standard sexual techniques, alternative methods, auxiliary paraphernalia, etc. I won't bore the reader with the now-boring particulars. By the 1960s, the famous Englishman could sing, "Why don't we do it in the road?"[1] Why not, indeed!

A quarter century later, Salt and Pepa (both of them) scored a massive hit by inviting Baby to "talk about sex"—including "*all* the good and the bad things."[2] And for the last few decades, the talk has grown only louder, more explicit, more relentless.

But—along the way—there've been unmistakable signs of uncandor, even shyness. New veils have appeared. New taboos have been quietly promulgated. These veils have obscured from sight facts with which our ancestors were casually, if not cheerfully, familiar.

---

1    John Lennon & Paul McCartney, *Why Don't We Do It in the Road?* (1968).
2    Salt-n-Pepa, *Let's Talk About Sex* (1990)

I'll here mention just one example. It involves a fact that is generally well known, but that became strangely obscure in recent decades. It's also somewhat amusing.

This fact is that men like women with a small waist and generous hips.

The veil covering this fact was famously torn off just one year after "Baby" was invited to talk about sex. We learned that "Baby" was "little in the middle" but had "much back." By this proclamation, Anthony Ray, who styled himself "Sir Mix-a-Lot," scored a double-platinum, Grammy-Award-winning single that has since become a part of Americana. It is probable that somewhere in America, at every hour, someone is playing the song.

The enduring success of the song cannot be attributed to its artistic quality. It's really not that good. Its popularity seems, instead, to have arisen from Ray's proclamation, with candid and bawdy humor, of a fact that was a *pleasing* revelation for many women: men actually like these particular curves.

As the composer himself explained, countless women expressed to him their *gratitude*. "About time!"[3] was the standard remark. For many women, the song was an epiphany: "Wow, men actually find my figure attractive."

For many women who lived through the 1970s and 1980s, with its celebration of "Twiggy" and other über-skinny figures, his blunt celebration of feminine abundance was refreshing, to say the least. Since the song's release, advertisers have made buckets of money from the same message. For years now, women's magazines have sold millions of copies by re-trumpeting the good "news" that curves are back in style. And just this past year, yet another songwriter scored a massive breakout hit by, in her words, "bringing booty back."[4]

The remarkable thing is that anyone has ever thought that "booty" needed to be brought "back." Back from where? For men at least, curves

---

3    Brian Keizer, "Big Buts," *Spin*, Sept. 1992, 87–88.
4    Meghan Trainor, *All About That Bass* (2014).

have never been out of style. It's "about time"? For male appetite, *any* time has been a good time, for men have *always* been "about that bass" (though without forsaking the treble). The memory of man runneth not to the contrary.

This "revelation" should be no revelation at all. Men's interest in curves is about as hardwired, ubiquitous, and unsurprising as kids' interest in sugar. Three hundred years ago, a Scottish poet celebrated his beloved's physique in nearly identical terms:

> She's backit like the peacock;
> She's breistit like the swan;
> She's jimp about the middle ;
> Her waist ye weel micht span:
> Her waist ye weel micht span,
> And she has a rolling eye;
> And for bonnie Annie Laurie
> I'll lay me doun and die.[5]

She was "jimp" in the middle, but she had much back—so much that she had the "back" of a peacock. But that's not all! As an added bonus, she was "breistit like the swan." My goodness.

Two hundred years ago, Jane Austen noted the same phenomenon, though in language at once both more muted and more amused: "Miss Bingley...got up and walked about the room. Her figure was elegant, and she walked well; but Darcy, at whom it was all aimed, was still inflexibly studious."

Miss Bingley invited first Miss Bennett and then Mr. Darcy, to join her in this promenade, but he refused with these words:

> "You either chuse this method of passing the evening because you are in each other's confidence, and have secret affairs to discuss, or because you are conscious that your figures appear to the greatest advantage in walking;—if the first, I should be completely in your way, and if the second, I can admire you much better as I sit by the fire."

---

5    William Douglas, *Maxwelton Banks* (c. 1700).

Now when you're sitting by the fire, watching all the girls go by, you're not supposed to say what you're doing. So in mock indignation, Miss Bingley playfully responded as follows: "Oh! shocking! I never heard any thing so abominable. How shall we punish him for such a speech?"[6]

The point is that at the beginning of the nineteenth century, everyone—including Miss Bennett, Miss Bingley, Mr. Darcy, Miss Austen, and her readers—all were in on the joke. At the end of that century, folks started taking the joke too far—with all the corsets and cartoonish bustles. Of course no one needed to sing, "I like big bustles, and I cannot lie." It was all too obvious.

Among the countless, more recent examples, consider P.G. Wodehouse's celebration of women with "as many curves as a scenic railway."[7] Or as Foghorn Leghorn, that famous white (and red-necked) rooster once said—more in sorrow than in anger—"Gal reminds me of a highway between Fort Worth & Dallas—no curves."[8] The pattern, across time and place, is unmistakable.[9]

A moment's reflection will suggest a reason for this almost-ubiquitous appetite. It's not about big butts, but big brains. As the ancient philosophers used to say, "man is a rational animal." Consequently, his appetite for reproduction looks toward the reproduction of rational, that is, smart animals. The modern biologist concurs: the premier evolutionary advantage of our species is intelligence. In turn, our animal rationality/evolved intelligence depends upon upright stature, big brains, and thus big heads.

This intelligence requires, in turn, that the potential mother have not only the upright stature but also the hips to bear some big-nogginned children. Male appetite says, "I want healthy smart kids, with their

---

6    Jane Austen, *Pride and Prejudice* (Mineola, NY: Dover Pubs. 2009), 37–38.

7    P.G. Wodehouse, *Mr. Mulliner Speaking* (New York: Overlook Press 2005), 9.

8    Warren Foster, *Of Rice and Hen* (1953).

9    If any reader seriously doubts this, I ask him or her to demand an honest answer from any heterosexual male under 40 as to whether he thinks he could go anywhere in the world, and know instantly which women's figures were deemed most attractive by the young men there.

upright stature and big brains." Men have, always and everywhere, liked seeing curvaceous women walk.[10]

My baby got back? The deeper meaning: my baby will get brains.[11]

So male appetite really, really, really, really wants healthy, intelligent offspring. The voice of nature, like the voice of men sometimes, is loud, monotonous, and kind of stupid. But nature, strangely enough, is often more noble, more decent, and less vulgar, than men.

How on earth could this basic fact of life have become unknown by the 1990s? Even after a century of all the crude, blunt "talk about sex," at least one basic, glaringly obvious, amusing fact about sex had become obscure to a significant number of people.

The reason for this blindness? I submit to the reader that, despite all our candor, we are, in some decisive respects, far more prudish than our ancestors. We cover with veils and outright lies not just the male interest in curves, but many other features of mutual attraction. These veils and lies make it hard for men and women to have the mutual understanding necessary to bond.

As I will discuss in the subsequent chapter, the leading cause for our prudishness about sex is our passion for equality. We love equality so much that we are embarrassed to think about, still less talk about, the stubbornly unequal facts of life. That is to say, our passion for equality makes us profoundly uncomfortable with natural passions, for Nature

---

10 Of course the voice of appetite is not necessarily the voice of conscious reason. Men and women may, of course, want the sex without the reproductive consequences, just as people frequently want to eat fat and sugar without the nutritional consequences. Still, both appetites seem to have a natural purpose: Just as the desire for food seems primarily (but not exclusively) about nourishing and preserving the body, sex seems primarily (but not exclusively) about cooperative reproduction. That original purpose abides in our appetites even if it's not our conscious purpose.

11 Indeed, contemporary research has found a correlation between a mother's lower waist-hip ratio and her offspring's higher cognitive ability. "Why is J.Lo so hot? Because males have a biological imperative to produce intelligent offspring, that's why." "The Brain/Butt Theory," *Chicago Tribune*, Nov. 18, 2007.

is most certainly not a democracy. But if we accept Nature, including her stubborn inequalities, we can have far greater success in the marital enterprise.

# CHAPTER TWO

## *WHY WE'VE FORGOTTEN: EQUALITY V. NATURE*

Equality. We live in a world deeply and peculiarly shaped by the ideal of equality. Equality is, in many ways, the mother of the modern world. As Lincoln observed, equality was the "proposition" to which America was "dedicated." Similarly, the French revolutionaries placed *"egalité"* right at the center of their slogan, with *"liberté"* and *"fraternité"* assigned merely supporting roles.

Equality has since triumphed around the world. Nearly all nations have adopted the Universal Declaration of Human Rights; its "cornerstone" and first principle is, "All human beings are born free and equal in dignity and rights."

This triumph of equality has yielded *enormous* benefits to humanity. In modern times, we've abolished slavery of different kinds and secured equal civil rights, equal political rights, and equality of all sorts, regardless of race, color, caste, religion, etc. We should never take these massive benefits for granted.

### A. Equality's Daily Pleasures

Equality, however, has become more than a political principle, more than a simple rule of justice. Equality has become a *passion*. This fact was best explained by the Frenchman Alexis de Tocqueville. Tocqueville came from French aristocratic lineage, but he was intensely interested in democracy, especially in America.

Writing nearly two centuries ago, he perceived that aristocracy was dying and democracy was rising, all around the world. America was at the cutting edge of this development. Equality was the wave of the future, and America was riding the crest.

Now Tocqueville was an aristocrat who liked to hang out with commoners, just as Sir Mix-a-Lot was a commoner who liked to play the aristocrat. While the latter told a little truth about one bodily passion (the love of small waists and whatnot), the former told many, deeper truths about our democratic passions.

Tocqueville emphasized that equality was indeed a *passion*. In a democratic society, people have a "love for equality" that is "ardent" and even "tenacious." This love is the "principal passion"—indeed the "singular and dominant fact" in democratic times.[1]

As he explained, we ardently love equality for several reasons. Not only is equality closely related to justice,[2] but equality gives us a variety of daily, easy pleasures. "Every day," Tocqueville wrote, "equality provides a multitude of little delights to every one." As a result, egalitarian passion is both "energetic and general," pervading the whole society.[3]

Equality's daily pleasures are threefold. First, equality relieves us of something annoying: the irritation, if not injustice, of having to treat anyone as a superior. Equality means we don't have to defer to some guy in a puffy shirt or bow before some pompous lady. Equality means that when you get in line for the movies, no snobbish jerk can cut to the front because of his S.A.T. scores, or his great-grandfather's

---

1    Alexis de Tocqueville, *De la Démocratie en Amérique* (Paris: Gallimard 1986), 2:137–138.

2    The philosopher Aristotle understood this well.

3    *Ibid.*, 140. In speaking of the daily little delights, Tocqueville uses the word *joissances*, which, not incidentally, is also the word for sexual climax. I am grateful to my colleague Professor Daniel Burns for this insight. As we'll note in this chapter, our fundamental difficulty is the incompatibility between sexual *joissance* and democratic *joissance*.

military exploits. Equality allows us to enjoy the simple dignity of non-inferiority; in the words of Aunt Eller in *Oklahoma!*, "I don't say I'm better than anybody else, But I'll be danged if I ain't just as good!"[4]

Second, equality makes social interactions a lot easier. In complex hierarchical societies, socializing can involve a steep learning curve. Interactions are governed by complex rules that depend on the relative class or caste of the persons. You bow deeply to this person, less deeply to that, tip your hat here, use different salutations, etc. Often aristocratic languages have two, three, or more words for "you," depending on the relative status of the speakers.[5] But equality gives us simplicity and informality: "Hi, I'm Dave" or perhaps even the monosyllabic "S'up?"

Third, for similar reasons, equality facilitates and preserves friendships. Hierarchies separate; they create a distance (however cordial) between the classes. Equality, in contrast, opens the door to friendly relations. As Tocqueville observed, in aristocratic times, the "general notion of common humanity is obscure," for people identify merely with their family, their class, their locality. But in democratic times, the concept of humanity becomes clearer, so the "bond of human affections extends and relaxes." Casual friendships thus become much easier across the lines of class, race, nationality, and even sex. Think of the easy coeducational camaraderie of the aptly named television show *Friends*.

Inequality can be harsh. In his memoirs, Jimmy Carter recalled powerfully how the racial-caste system of his Georgia boyhood undermined his childhood friendships. As a youngster, his closest friends were a group of black boys. But when Carter was fourteen years old (in 1938), something happened that spoiled this easy camaraderie:

> One day about this time, [we] approached the gate leading from our barn to the pasture. To my surprise, they opened it and stepped back to let me go through first…It was a small act, but a deeply symbolic one. After that, they often treated me with some deference. I guess that their parents had done or said something that caused this change

---

  4   Oscar Hammerstein II, *Oklahoma!* (1943).

  5   Consider, for instance, the difference in Spanish addressing someone as "*tu*" or "*usted*."

in my black friends' attitude. [A] precious sense of equality had gone out of our personal relationship, and things were never again the same between them and me.[6]

Inequality, then, obstructs and even destroys friendships.

In sum, equality is *fairer*. It's easier and kinder. Equality is good. Of course we do not simply *believe in* equality. We *like* it—we like it a lot.

## B. Equality's Failures

Nonetheless, no matter how much we love equality, inequality remains a persistent, stubborn fact of life. As Lincoln said, all men are created equal, but only with respect to the basic rights of life, liberty, etc. We are plainly not equal in other respects, such as "size, intellect, moral development, or social capacity."[7] There is obvious inequality in intelligence, beauty, health, wealth, etc.

More scandalously, most of this inequality does not seem very just. It's largely beyond our control; success often requires just dumb luck.[8] To be sure, sometimes *merit* plays a role, but even then, it's hard to discern exactly where merit begins and luck ends. For instance, to work hard is meritorious, and such hard work often results in more wealth, but to be hardworking is a habit, and acquiring this habit often depends on the luck of good genetics and/or good parents.

So with a little bit of pluck and a whole lot of luck, people become grossly unequal, especially in wealth, fame, friendships, looks, etc. We may love our equality today, but everywhere we see glaring inequality.

This inequality is especially problematic in two areas: money and sex. In our times, economic inequality is obvious, massive, and growing.

6    Jimmy Carter, *An Hour Before Daylight: Memories of a Rural Boyhood* (New York: Simon & Schuster 2001), 229.

7    Reply of Lincoln at the Lincoln-Douglas Debate at Alton, IL (1858).

8    Some of my religious readers may say that "Providence" not "luck" is the best term for this phenomenon. While I agree, it seems plain that at first glance, or maybe even at second glance, that the face on this wild card of life looks more like the god "Dumb Luck" than the face of an all-loving Father. This book is about common sense, not faith.

But beauty inequality is no less prevalent. Some women are just more beautiful than others. Some men are just more attractive than others. If you are a woman reading this book, it is almost certain that you are *far* less pretty than Halle Berry or Natalie Portman. If you are a man reading this book, George Clooney outranks and outclasses you in women's eyes—by a massive margin.

These inequalities of sex and money are often interrelated. In a popular ballad, the Tejana star Selena claimed that "Money doesn't matter to you, or to me, or to the heart."[9] But that's really not true. Women seem to like richer men—sometimes a lot more. Ask a rich man who was once poor. Economic inequality makes women unequally attractive as well. Wealth may not directly make a woman more appealing, but it provides the money and leisure time to spend on skin care, exercise, clothes, etc. Ask a single mom working two jobs.

It gets worse. Not only are we unequal, but so many of us are decidedly inferior. Remember that exactly 50% of people are below average. On a scale of 1-10, most of us are at 5 or below—and many of us down around 1, 2 or 3. Stated otherwise, we get a C, a D, maybe even a D- or worse. For most of us, mediocrity (or worse) is our lot in life.

Sexual inequality is particularly offensive to our passion for equality. It's bad enough that men and women clearly discriminate on the basis of looks, height, and the like—that is, on grounds unrelated to merit or virtue. But the sexes themselves are *unequally unequal*. Men seemingly discriminate more on the basis of the shape of the figure, but women on the basis of height, for instance. Moreover, as we will elaborate in a later chapter, there's another embarrassing fact: one of the sexes ranks the other according to a less forgiving, much steeper hierarchy; that is, in our democratic times, one sex has appetites that are more *aristocratic*.

Even worse, sexual inequality piles embarrassment and guilt on top of disappointment. If we're honest, we see our own complicity. The disappointed man may denounce women as snobs, but he too is a snob,

---

9    "El dinero no importa en ti ni en mi, ni en el corazón." Selena Quintanilla & A.B. Quintanilla III, *Amor Prohibido* (1994).

discriminating in favor of the youthful and shapely. A woman might complain about male superficiality, but then remembers that she herself likes tall guys and spurns the short. I once read of a woman once wrote, with candor and a bit of contrition, "Okay call me shallow—but I prefer tall men...I'm sorry, short men. But that's how I'm programmed. I'm part of the problem, but I can't help it."

For the religious, this shame can be particularly acute. The major world faiths tend emphatically to reject, even invert, some of these hierarchies. A Christian woman might hear "Blessed are the poor," and "Blessed are the meek,"[10] and say, "Amen." But her desire responds, "Maybe so, but when dating, I'll just stick with the rich, brave, and bold. I kind of like the man on horseback, not the beggar in the ditch. But thanks for the suggestion." Likewise a young Jewish man might piously read that "charm is deceitful, and beauty is vain."[11] But his appetite retorts, "If that's so, then I'd rather have a second helping of this deceit and vanity. *Please*."

Finally, of course, these stubborn inequalities can be painfully disappointing. Many men and women come to the quiet bitter conclusion that they are hopelessly attracted to the opposite sex, but the opposite sex is hopelessly unattracted to them. Unrequited affection is their brutal lot in life.

## C. Grieving for Equality

At a deeply personal level, then, our aristocratic natures vanquish our democratic desires. Confronted with this stubborn, ugly, unequal reality, our egalitarian ideal perishes. We face the death of a loved one.

When facing such death, according to Elisabeth Kübler-Ross's famous model, there are five stages of grief: (1) denial, (2) anger, (3) bargaining, (4) depression and (5) acceptance. So where are we in the grieving process?

---

10  Matt. 5:3–5.
11  Prov. 31:30.

## 1. Our Denial

Our culture is mostly stuck on denial. This denial takes several forms. First we deny by silence. It's gauche to refer bluntly to the undemocratic facts: that men seem to prefer youthful beauty or that women seem to like the taller, stronger, wealthier, etc. So we remain silent.

In this regard, democratic denial surely played a part in creating the veil that Sir Mix-a-Lot tore off. To celebrate childbearing hips is one step away from celebrating childbearing. But to celebrate childbearing is to highlight the very realm where the sexes are undeniably unequal: men only sire offspring; men can't get pregnant, but the vast majority of women can.[12] Not surprisingly, our culture veiled childbearing hips precisely when the culture's passion for gender equality was greatest, e.g., in the 1920s and the 1970s. Conversely, when such passion was less intense, e.g., in the 1890s or 1950s or 1990s, the hourglass re-emerged in glorious triumph.

Second, we deny by pleasant egalitarian myths.[13] We say "everyone is equally beautiful." Or, for much the same purpose, we adopt the opposite myth: all are equal because beauty does not really exist. Beauty, we say, is transient, artificial, if not insubstantial, existing as either a social construct or, alternatively, in the "eye of the beholder."[14]

Another egalitarian untruth, earnestly proclaimed, is that "there is someone out there for everybody." That's just not true. Millions of people seek marriage but never find it.

The ultimate egalitarian myth is the assertion of radical agnosticism. It's all a mystery, we hear. Attraction is unknowable—it's mysterious and /

---

12  As to the question of which sex gets the better deal, the answer depends on one's perspective. For those who do not desire offspring, childbearing capacity is a massive burden. For those who do desire offspring, childbearing is better insofar as that parent has a more intimate and secure relation with the child. Stated simply, if babies are good, women probably are the superior sex.

13  Does anyone *really* believe these myths are actually true?

14  I have not heard anyone combine these two myths: such that society (violently) imposes its constructions on our eyeballs.

or unpredictable. "And therefore is winged Cupid painted blind."[15] At best, this assertion is a half truth. Attraction is, in some major part, plainly predictable. Ask a now-slender woman who once weighed 300 pounds.[16] Ask a short rich man who was once very poor.[17]

Third, we deny by outright denial. We pronounce ourselves indifferent to the flesh. Instead, we say, we care about the personality, character, spiritual stuff, but not such concerns as looks, money, or the like. *We're* not superficial or shallow; we don't discriminate like that. We're too noble. We say, for instance, "Let us leave pretty women to men with no imagination."[18]

One sees a similar pattern of denial in the realm of money. The economist George Gilder explained this phenomenon well:

> [Mo]ney has become the "dirty little secret" of American life... There are few rules of etiquette so firm as the ban on boasting about salary and income or on confessing the financial spurs and influences in our behavior....And never do we brandish our wealth so rawly as when we declare it means nothing to us, that "it's more trouble than it's worth."... Our response to the social pressures of money is a tendency by everyone to pretend to be "middle class" and from a "modest" background.[19]

As Gilder emphasized, this "mask of manners and hypocrisies" is quite helpful in "softening envy and conflict"; we thereby "protect one another from the rough edges of perennial social struggle." Candor about such unequal matters is painful and unkind, especially in our democratic age.

---

15  William Shakespeare, *A Midsummer Night's Dream*, act 1, sc. 1., line 235.

16  If Cupid's arrow were indiscriminate, it would hit the larger target with more frequency.

17  As one can imagine, if the sexes are unequally aristocratic—then the need to conceal or deny will be greater. The sex with more aristocratic appetites will profess these egalitarian fictions with greater frequency and fervor.

18  Marcel Proust, *The Captive; The Fugitive* (New York: The Modern Library 2003), 592.

19  George Gilder, *Wealth and Poverty* (Washington, D.C.: Regnery Publishing 2012), 126–128.

But, as he further notes, this veiling and deception "has the further effect of distorting many people's views of the very nature of the society."[20] In other words, after a while, we deceive ourselves by starting to believe our own bulls—t. The persistent pretension to equality softens our social interactions, but also our brains.

### 2. Our Anger

Where denial is impossible or unhelpful, the next available option is anger. Angry men will call women "snobs," "gold-diggers," or worse. Disappointed women will call men "shallow," "superficial" and "pigs." We accuse, we blame the other sex. Their bad will or malice *must* be the cause of our rejection.

Surprisingly, this exasperation affects even professional matchmakers. I once heard a long-time dating coach say, with obvious disdain, that she had never had a male client who didn't prioritize a woman's beauty. Conversely, a male veteran complained that in his experience, women, even short women, rejected short men. These "hypocrites," he wrote, displayed "all the shallowness and superficiality that they love to accuse men of possessing." Even after decades in the business, these professionals were still annoyed by their (opposite-sex) clients.

Now a little reflection can sometimes curb this indignation. The thoughtful might realize that both sexes are complicit in the crime against equality: both are undemocratic and even anti-meritocratic. The guilt of all should be the innocence of all.

A bit more reflection acquits both sides of the charge of malice. Women don't *choose* to prefer taller men, nor do men willfully decide to like the young and curvy. It's a matter of unchosen, stubborn appetite.

But egalitarian indignation demands a scapegoat. If the opposite sex isn't to blame, then the remaining candidates seem to be advertisers, corporations, or most conveniently,[21] the impersonal "society."

---

20  *Ibid.*

21  It's convenient because one does not have to engage in the inequalitarian business of blaming anyone in particular.

Yet even this indictment proves unpersuasive. There's little evidence that society manufactured male or female desire. No secret club *decided* that women must prefer the tall and handsome. No nefarious elite *selected* the curvaceous as pleasing to men. To be sure, advertising can have some influence on desire, but only at the margins. No marketing campaign could *ever* convince men to prefer a fat-necked, flat-chested shape instead of the hourglass, or make women go weak in the knees when a nice, short, poor guy walks in the room.

### 3. Our Depression

After anger— whether at "society," at the other sex, or at our own sorry selves— there is depression. We long for marital love, but we're just not lovable. The singer "learned the truth at seventeen, that love was meant for beauty queens."[22] Nobody's to blame, except maybe Nature, or Fate, or God.

Many, many people, both male and female, feel this pain. They have a deep, honest, undeniable longing to love and be loved by a member of the opposite sex. Yet, it seems, this affection, no matter how sincere— will NOT be requited.

This sentiment, of course, becomes a self-fulfilling prophesy—an iron-clad destiny. Confidence and action collapse.

---

Whether in denial, anger, or depression, the sexes are mutually alienated. Consequently, "distrust suffuses the apparently easy commerce between the sexes."[23] It all seems very grim and not very playful.

But what if this distrust is wrongheaded? What if the truth about men and women is much kinder—that the "commerce" between the sexes can and should be so much *easier*? As I'll elaborate in the next few chapters, our egalitarian passions—and grief—should be faced down

22  Janis Ian, *At Seventeen* (1974).

23  Allan Bloom, *Closing of the American Mind* (New York: Simon & Schuster 1988), 124.

and shoved aside. As Tennyson said in his poem on men and women, "equal" is our "proud watchword," that must be put to "rest."[24] Our love of equality hides a reality that is far more promising and hopeful to the marriage minded, and thus to the future of civilization.

---

24  Alfred Lord Tennyson, *The Princess* (1847).

# CHAPTER THREE

## *HOW TO PROCEED: PAST ACCEPTANCE...AND ONWARD TO ACTION*

The purpose of this book is to encourage those who want to get married. I did not write this book for those who like to wallow, whether in denial, anger, or depression. I wrote this book for the enterprising, the go-getters—for those who want to move forward, to take action. They dream, but with determination.[1]

And so, onward!

We're told that the last stage of grief is acceptance; that is, something peaceful, quiet, serene. For those wanting to get married, acceptance isn't very helpful. You don't get married by loitering. A husband or wife doesn't appear out of nowhere at your doorstep, still less through your bedroom window. Even if that someone is the proverbial boy or girl next door, you still have to go next door. Getting married requires not quiet *acceptance* but *action*.

---

1    In this regard, I can't help but think of the lyric found in the French version of the Disney film "Sleeping Beauty," and the song "Once Upon a Dream." Aurora sings,
*Refusons tous deux que nos lendemains soient mornes et gris*
*Nous attendrons l'heure de notre bonheur*
That is: "Let us refuse to accept that our tomorrow should be sad and gray; instead, we'll await the hour of our happiness." A fierce optimism is the recipe. Natacha Nahon, *J'en ai Rêvé* (1959) (adaptation of Sammy Fain & Jack Lawrence, *Once Upon a Dream* (1959)).

Our goal here is to push forward, to move beyond denial, anger, and depression. We aim to break through acceptance into action—even successful action.

How we should proceed? In setting our course, we'll rely upon our modern character, especially the modern American character.

In the last chapter, I discussed how much the modern person loves equality—and rightly so. Unfortunately, such a love can be so intense as to blind us to the unequal facts of life, so it's not ultimately helpful to us in this enterprise.

But we have other tendencies that are favorable to our enterprise here: *candor, humor,* and *kindness.* We like to face facts, to tell it like it is, to keep it real. Further, we like to laugh. And we like to be nice to each other.

In the subsequent chapters, then, I intend to lay out the unequal truths about sexual and marital attraction, with candor but good-natured humor, with an eye toward promoting mutual understanding and good feeling. Men and women can't get hitched if they don't understand and like each other. And along the way, we can laugh at ourselves.

Now some may object that laughter isn't good medicine—that laughter about marriage and sex is too crude and frivolous to help men and women get hitched. To be sure, bawdy humor can be so coarse and disgusting as to repel the imagination and the heart. And marriage is a serious thing, after all.

But paradoxically, the only way to take sex and marriage seriously is to laugh at it. You can't view the topic with any honesty if you don't see the absurdities of it all. Consider breasts, if I may, and if you will. Now breasts are important. Before the domestication of certain animals, breasts were absolutely necessary to our survival; and even today, breastfeeding is very conducive to the health of babies and the mother-child relationship.

Yet boobies are also funny, and men's fascination with them is even funnier. The fact that a magazine called "Juggz" ever existed, let alone dominate the porno-mag market, is an interesting fact. But the best and healthiest response to this fact is laughter.

Speaking more generally, erotic desire is ridiculous. Although at times it seems so transcendent, a "many splendored thing," sometimes it's as dumb as flesh. The novelist C.S. Lewis explained this absurdity well:

> I can hardly help regarding it as one of God's jokes, that a passion so soaring, so apparently transcendent as Eros should be thus linked in incongruous symbiosis with a bodily appetite, which, like any other appetite, tactlessly reveals its connections with such mundane factors as weather, health, diet, circulation and digestion. In Eros at times we seem to be flying; Venus gives us the sudden twitch that reminds us we are really captive balloons. It is a continual demonstration of the truth that we are composite creatures, rational animals, akin on one side to the angels, on the other to tom-cats.[2]

So let's proceed with resolution, candor, and a sense of humor.

---

2   C.S. Lewis, *The Four Loves, in* Amy A. Kass and Leon R. Kass, eds., *Wing to Wing, Oar to Oar: Readings on Courting and Marrying* (Notre Dame, IN: University of Notre Dame Press, 2000), 293.

# CHAPTER FOUR

## WHAT WE'VE FORGOTTEN: NATURE'S STUBBORN HARD FACTS

L et's get this over with.

In this chapter, we'll dig into some "hard" unpleasant facts. They're unpleasant primarily because they do violence to our egalitarian passions.

In this area, "a little learning is a dangerous thing." The poet Alexander Pope famously began a couplet with those words. He elaborated as follows:

> A little learning is a dangerous thing ;
> Drink deep, or taste not the Pierian spring :
> There shallow draughts intoxicate the brain,
> And drinking largely sobers us again.[1]

The problem in our subject, however, is that here a little learning will not *intoxicate* but *anger* and *demoralize*. In our times, this effect just aggravates the mutual alienation between the sexes. The first glance can depress. It is the second and third look that, I believe, gives reason for hope, and even play. But first we need an initial candid look at the unequal truths.

Therefore, I ask you to read this "hard" chapter only if you commit yourself to reading the next "hopeful" chapter. I wrote this book to

---

1    Alexander Pope, *An Essay on Criticism* (1711).

encourage, not demoralize.

## A. Recovering Common Sense: Limitations and Method

The recovery of common sense will first involve a review of some facts about male and female appetite. These facts will be similar to the following kind of claim:

On average and in general, children like candy.

How far is this true, and how do we know it's true?

First, let's consider how *limited* these claims are. These statements are not *comprehensive* of all individuals on the planet. They are not absolute universals; to say that kids like candy does not mean that *each* and *every* child likes candy, and still less that every child *should* or *must* like candy.

We understand this statement simply to mean that the vast majority of kids just like candy, and this generalization is particularly helpful if one is planning something, like a party, designed to please kids. Similarly, if one is planning something like finding a spouse, one should be familiar with what the vast majority of eligible men and women find appealing.

In addition to being limited, these types of assertions are also not *inclusive* of all the important things related to the appetites, whether we're discussing eating or sex. There are a variety of factors that contribute to marital attraction, much as there are many factors that would make a dinner party a success. But the brute, stubborn facts of our taste for fat and sugar are not unimportant. A dinner party, even with the finest china, guests, conversation, would be a failure if the hostess served nothing but the healthiest of steamed broccoli on the finest china. Similarly, the marital pursuit will be disastrous if men and women overlook or deny the stubborn facts of sexual appetite.

Second, we know this claim is true by the common sense that comes primarily from personal experience. That is, we already know this truth because of a lifetime of experience: experience of our own appetites as children and the experience observing others' appetites. Even if we are among the small minority who never liked candy, we have seen plenty of evidence supporting the claim that children, on average and in general, like candy a lot.

We know this claim is true *not* because the claim has been subject to a battery of double-blind peer-reviewed scientific studies. Indeed, even if some institution should undertake an expensive, elaborate study on children and candy, the conclusions could not really improve upon our experiential knowledge.

Besides honest reflection on personal experience, there are at least three other ways we can recover common sense in the matter of sex and marriage. First, we can rely on the experiential knowledge of those with marital success, who got and stayed married for a long time—that is, the old wives and husbands. Second, we can rely on the experiential knowledge reflected in literature that has sustained a reputation across generations—thus having been ratified by the judgment of generations of men and women. In matrimonial affairs, I think Jane Austen is the best guide. Third, we can engage in what I call "paleo-thinking"—by recalling that humanity is millions of years old, and that sex and sexual desire were shaped by millions of years of evolution, almost all of which occurred before modern technology, and even before the invention of agriculture and metallurgy.

By thus relying on personal and vicarious experience, informed by a little science, we can hope to recover what Alexander Hamilton once called "the natural and unsophisticated dictates of common-sense."[2] Yet the only way we learn is if we put aside prejudice, anger, etc. and candidly look at experience. Be honest. Tell the truth.

**B. The Great Sex Divide (or Nature's Great Sin Against Equality)**

Let's get to it.

The desire for sex is, first and foremost, an appetite. It is, in this respect, like the appetite for food. As anyone who's been on a diet will report, the appetite for food has a stubborn, stupid character to it. So, too, does the appetite for sex.

---

2    Federalist Papers No. 31.

Like the appetite for food, the appetite for sex seems, by its very nature, designed to serve certain natural purposes. Just as the first natural end of eating appears to be nutrition, the first natural end of sex appears to be the generation of offspring. Of course, these primary ends are not necessarily conscious or desired; indeed the participants, whether eating or copulating, usually do not think about nutrition or reproduction, and may be hoping for the opposite. That is, they frequently desire to enjoy the pleasure but avoid the natural result— whether the digestion of calories or the making of babies.[3] Moreover, this primary end is far from the *only* purpose of these appetites. Apart from their sheer pleasure, both food and sex serve a complex variety of personal and social purposes.[4]

There is, however, at least one stark difference between the appetite for food and sex. The appetite for sex is far more problematic in our democratic times because it involves some *stark-naked inequalities*.

In several respects, the sexes are plainly equal. First, there is a perfect equality in one respect: every human being on the planet is a result of countless, millions of male-female bonds. Each of us, male and female, is equally a male-female construct. And in our lineage, there is perfect gender equality: each of those bonds included precisely an equal number of male and female participants (one each), and in each bond, the participation of both male and female was equally necessary. Second, men and women both are mortal. We both have the same destination—death (though some get there faster than others). Third, along the way, men and women have desires that incline them to the same destination: offspring.

But bonding and breeding are suffused with massive inequalities. First and foremost, the resulting offspring themselves are shocking reminders that our chief egalitarian myth is just false, that human beings are not

---

3    The fact that eating and sex are, by nature, for nutrition and offspring does not necessarily imply any moral obligation to pursue these ends. Nature is not necessarily an *authority*, unless, perhaps, Nature has an *Author*.

4    For an interesting account of the multiple purposes and functions of eating, see Leon Kass's book, *The Hungry Soul: Eating and the Perfecting of Our Nature* (1999).

born "equal and independent." Babies are naked—nakedly *unequal* vis-à-vis adults and nakedly *dependent* upon them.

But offspring involve another stark inequality: the sexes are scandalously unequal in their relation to offspring. Women bear, men sire: <u>Nature's great sin</u> against gender equality.

This great inequality is the parent of at least <u>three</u> inequalities. The first concerns the *burden* of offspring. Men show up for the fun part, but then the burden, the pains, the labor are all foisted on the women. And for much of human history, childbirth was not merely burdensome, but a leading cause of death, leaving women with a much shorter life expectancy.

The second concerns the *number* of offspring. Although Nature gives both men and women millions of gametes, men can potentially sire *thousands* of offspring while women can bear, at most, a dozen or two. And for much of human history, women would bury half of their children before the age of five.

There's a wise old saying: "Don't put all your eggs in one basket." But Nature has shoved this folly onto woman. All her eggs *are* in one basket—her own body.

But there is a third inequality no less stark, and it involves the *identity* of offspring. The fact that the woman's sole basket is her very body gives her near-perfect security that her child is her own. But men, by nature, have no basis for such confidence.[5]

In sum, women bear the burden of offspring and can have only a small number of them. Women can be nearly certain as to the identity of their own offspring. Men are much freer to sow the seed but deeply insecure as to whether what they might reap (and raise) are what they've sown.

To be sure, (very) modern technology softens these inequities considerably. Improved contraceptive devices make it easier to engage in sex but avoid pregnancy. Improved obstetrics make pregnancy

---

5   Women themselves are not always sure as to the father's identity.

(and especially childbirth) less laborious and less dangerous. Modern genetic testing, in turn, makes men less unequal to women as to identifying offspring. In the coming century, the likely invention of artificial wombs would further promote this equality of the sexes, for good or for bad. Women will no longer have to bear offspring, and men will no longer need to rely on women's bodies: technology could, to a point, mutually liberate the sexes from one another and make them more equal vis-à-vis offspring.[6]

But stubborn inequalities remain. The biggest problem is this: our appetites are millions of years old and don't care very much about what has happened in the last few centuries. Our appetite for sex is deeply shaped by the inequalities—shaped by thousands and thousands of generation of evolution, when these technologies were unavailable.

As far as our appetites are concerned, it's like the last few generations never happened. This massive discrepancy between technological progress and our stubborn old appetites occurs in eating: on average and in general, people crave concentrated forms of fat and sugar as if times of scarcity were probable, even though modern technology has largely overcome this scarcity. Every person who's ever been on a diet knows this: you can tell your body not to worry about the coming famine, but the body doesn't listen.[7] We tell our bodies: "Don't worry—those seven lean years aren't coming." And the body replies, "Right, pal. I've heard that one before, and I won't be fooled again. I'm storin' up."

Similarly, the sexual appetite, then, remains oriented toward offspring. The members of both sexes are hardwired to produce offspring who can survive to adulthood. But the sexes have radically different relations to offspring, and thus have unequal approaches to sex. Let's review these radically different desires—the foundation of mutual attraction.

---

6    Whether these changes are good or not is a different question. For good or for bad, I suspect that the sheer existence of this technology to facilitate more and different reproductive modes will actually result in far less reproduction overall.

7    Childhood obesity, it is said, is our primary nutritional challenge. For most of human history, however, parents often *prayed* for that problem.

## C. What Women Like

*"Are you, by any chance, looking at me as a matrimonial prospect?"*[8]

### 1. Strength

Because Nature forced the woman to put all her eggs in one basket—her own body—she is naturally very protective of those eggs, and rather selective as to whom she allows to fertilize them. What do women want in a fertility partner? *Strength*.

Sex is reproduction—but the goal isn't babies, it's other adults, with all that intelligence. Pregnancy is hard, but it's much harder to raise a baby to adulthood. It takes a lot of energy and other resources. Children are so labor-intensive: they need so, so much, not only in the way of food, water, and shelter, but in attention, care, and education. Ask any mother.

Women by nature, then, are looking for something: *help!* They are looking for a man with not only genetic health but *resources*. Women prefer not only healthy men, but taller men, more muscular men, richer men, smarter men, more talented men, and more confident men. Each of these qualities is a kind of strength. These men have, or appear to have, the resources that will be critical to the success of her (and his) offspring.

A man with all these strengths has hit the jackpot. Consider Mr. Darcy, when he first swaggers onto the scene in *Pride and Prejudice*: Although Mr. Bingley was quite handsome and wealthy, "his friend Mr. Darcy soon drew the attention of the room by his fine, tall person, handsome features, noble mien; and the report which was in general circulation within five minutes after his entrance, of his having ten thousand a year.... [T]he ladies declared he was much handsomer than [his friend], and he was looked at with great admiration for about half the evening."[9]

---

8  Warren Foster, *Of Rice and Hen* (1953).
9  Jane Austen, *Pride and Prejudice* (Mineola, NY: Dover Pubs. 2009), 6.

Darcy was tall, rich, and cocksure: he hit the trifecta. Almost anytime you find a man that many women find attractive, that man will almost always have one, and usually two or more, prominent strengths, whether actual or perceived. Darcy had at least three.

The evidence for this appetite for strength seems to be everywhere. One place to look is the market, for there, knowledge about appetite gets you rich; as a result, commerce often exposes the candid truth about appetite, despite all our democratic myths.

By"market", I'm not referring to the relatively small gigolo market, nor the growing sperm-donor market (though in both these cases, strength of body and/or mind is surely a requirement for male success). Rather, I'm thinking of the far more lucrative areas of romance novels and romantic comedies. Survey the advertisements and cover art: over and over and over again, the physically strong and confident man dominates. Frequently too, the man appears to be economically or socially strong.

Of course, women consciously like other qualities besides strength. Women reasonably like men to be kind, patient, respectful, etc., etc., etc. And women are far more likely to mention these attributes. But at a foundational, subrational level, strength is the key. A man lacking any strength of body, mind, wallet, or personality, will find it very, very, very difficult to attract women, no matter how kind or sweet or sensitive he is.

Consider, among countless examples, how the ladies sing the praises of a man in the musical, *The Pajama Game*:

> *Well of course you've noticed his manly physique and that look in his eye.*
> *Well I'm sure he can cut almost any man out of size!*
> *He must he as fierce as a tiger when he's mad*
> *And I'll bet he cries like a little boy when he's sad.*[10]

So women do like men who can cry, *but with one massive proviso*: he must first be strong—with the manly physique, the look, the superior

---

10  Richard Adler & Jerry Ross, *Pajama Game* (1954).

strength, the fierceness.[11] Then, and only then, may he have the occasional tear in his eye as a cute accessory. Women like strong men who cry; a weak man who cries is just a crybaby, unfit for even the Friend zone.

Again, take a look at the titles of the romance novels or romantic comedies. You will find none titled *The Listener*, still less any entitled *Five-foot Two, Eyes of Blue*.[12] You will, however, find such unrestrained titles as *The Billionaire's Bridal Bargain* and *Pregnant by the Sheikh*.

And don't be fooled by the word "cute." Women do not like "cute" men. The word represents a great democratic lie that women tell themselves and other to veil their incurably aristocratic appetites. Bunnies are cute. Attractive men are not.

Now to say that women like strength is to say that women have aristocratic appetites. And in our democratic times, the claim sounds like an accusation. But I mean it as a simple statement of fact without any assignment of blame or guilt. Indeed, women can't help it—they're hardwired that way.

But because of our passion for equality, women are very reluctant to think, let alone mention, this truth. If asked, in our democratic times, what they find attractive in men, they'll describe any number of non-aristocratic features or traits, but frequently avoid anything like "strength." But in truth, almost any time a woman today expresses a preference for anything, including sensitivity, tenderness, etc., etc. she is thinking of a man she already likes—because of his strength.

---

11 It's in the Bible too: "His hands are as gold rings set with the beryl: his belly is as bright ivory overlaid with sapphires. His legs are as pillars of marble, set upon sockets of fine gold: his countenance is as Lebanon, excellent as the cedars. His mouth is most sweet: yea, he is altogether lovely. This is my beloved, and this is my friend, O daughters of Jerusalem." Song of Sol. 5:14–16. First a man needs the strength—the legs like pillars, the face with the power of cedar trees; only then is the sweetness of his mouth all that interesting to the daughters of Jerusalem, or the daughters of the whole Earth, for that matter.

12 If such titles do exist, the short persons and the listener almost certainly identify the woman, not the man.

After all, in the word "gentleman," *man* is the noun, the foundation, while *gentle* the mere adjective. The attractive gentleman displays not male-flavored gentleness, but gentle manliness.

There is, however, one exception to women's lack of candor as to strength—and here too, democratic passions explain the exception. Women on average and in general like taller men, and are usually not shy about it. And here too the market doesn't lie: the massive relationship website Eharmony learned this truth hard way when its female customers complained so frequently at being matched with shorter men. Eharmony responded by changing its formula to appease the customers.[13] The reason for women's candor: the height preference does not offend our egalitarian passions but partly confirms them, for everyone knows that men rate women by their physical appearances, so women's height preference (and other looks preferences) can and should be emphasized precisely to show women's equality with men.[14] Women's plainly aristocratic preference for wealth and social standing, however, are more embarrassing, for they have no analogue in male appetites.

Many men are unfair to women in this regard. Men will notice women's preference for the rich, the tall, and the confident. Men—especially the poorer, the shorter, the less confident—get angry and hurl accusations: women are gold-diggers, women are snobs, etc. This mistaken anger is understandable: democratic men assume that women are equal to men, and men know that if they pursued women for money, the pursuit would come not from appetite but calculation. Men reasonably conclude, in our democratic times, that women's attraction to wealth and power must be similarly calculated.

To be sure, women *are* sometimes calculating, and often (but not always)

---

13  Valerie Reitman, "We Clicked," *Los Angeles Times*, Apr. 26, 2004.

14  The egalitarianism can be misleading, as *some* women are prone to speak rather bluntly about men's physiques and body parts in a manner consciously imitative of men. Men who hear the frequency and vulgarity of such comments are often misled into thinking that women *equally* prioritize these matters. Believe me: a six-figure salary will go much, much further with women than six-pack abs.

for good reason.[15] But in most respects, women are attracted to wealth as a matter of uncalculated appetite. Wealth, like other strengths, has a magnetic influence on women's subrational sexual and matrimonial desires. Even very wealthy women, who have no conscious need or desire for more money, are drawn to the wealthy man.

Women's attraction to *strength* largely explains a widespread misunderstood phenomenon that really makes the sexes dislike one another:

*The Bad-Boy Half-Truth.*

Men frequently observe the very common phenomenon: If you meet an arrogant, haughty, entitled, somewhat anti-social man, he very frequently has an attractive, adoring woman on his arm. Oftentimes this man is unkind and obnoxious not only to people in general, but to the woman herself. Almost all men believe this phenomenon is widespread; many women silently concur; and some women will even candidly say so.

This fact makes women and men dislike each other, but in different ways. Women who repeatedly enter these relationships get hurt, and understandably develop an angry, mistrustful attitude toward men in general; such women see themselves as moths and men as malicious flames.

Even more so, the proverbial nice guy gets angry at women. From his childhood, women taught him to be kind and considerate. Well into adulthood, other women told him to be kind and considerate—that "real men respect women," etc., etc., *ad nauseam*. And this message made sense to him. A good democrat, he believed that men and women were equal, and he knew that he and his friends liked nice women— so of course women would like nice, pleasant men, and he planned accordingly. Yet then he learned the (apparent) bitter truth: women like

---

15  A woman who is planning on having a child or even children has good reason to chose a husband partly based on his current or likely earnings. Children are very expensive, especially while young, in part because they are so labor-intensive that it's hard for both parents to maintain full-time jobs.

jerks. He consequently feels betrayed by women, and, even worse, by democracy. "Women like jerks! But I'm not a jerk. I don't want to be a jerk. And even if I wanted to, I'm now impotent, incapable of being a jerk—thanks to a lifetime of female indoctrination!"

The angry nice guy is mistaken. Women don't like jerks, *per se*. They like strength. The "bad boy" attracts by giving an *illusion* of strength by his hubris and his apparent ability to flout convention and still survive, if not flourish. He's much like the peacock who is "hot" because he has a massive colorful tail; the tail is a handicap, making him vulnerable to predators, so his very survival is a testimony to his strength. The peacock is the ultimate bad-ass (or more specifically bad-tail), and the peahens love him for it—not the tail itself but the strength indicated by his survival despite the handicap. Similarly, it is not the *bad*ness of the bad boy that attracts some women; it's the strength his badness suggests.[16]

In truth, women generally like kind, gentle strength, but if they have to choose, they like the strength over the kindness, especially if the bad-boy is kind to them at least. Moreover, most women are sensible enough to consciously avoid the bad boy; they prudently prioritize kindness despite their appetites, much as the average man wisely avoids the crazy hot girl. Most women seek male strength in other, less dangerous, more sociable forms.

Still, a substantial minority number of women are foolish enough to let their hormones get the best of them. Our egalitarian passions may be the cause for this peculiarly female fault. The love of equality alienates women from their aristocratic appetites. Instead a veil is placed over the whole matter, and women instead will attribute their affection to "mystery" or "destiny" or "chemistry," but never to the true source: naked biochemistry, an appetite that is no more transcendent than

---

16  A minority of the women who like bad men do so for other reasons. Some women were so badly abused or neglected by their fathers that they confuse love with abuse. Some women are attracted to the drama of the relationship; they don't like the pain, but they love the roller-coaster ride. But among the women who do like the bad boy, most are simply attracted to his apparent strength.

men's attraction to breasts.[17] Once unidentified, the female appetite becomes less governable.

Homer, in his *Odyssey*, tells us this truth through the tale of the god Hephaestus. Hephaestus is a "nice guy" as far as gods go: he's a hardworking, reliable god. A sensible father, Zeus decided to give his beautiful daughter Aphrodite in marriage to this nice guy god. But there's a problem: Hephaestus was weak, having been born lame. Not surprisingly, while her dad liked the nice god, Aphrodite liked the hot (i.e., strong) gods, and shared her bodily affections with the god of war Ares. Upon discovering the adultery, Hephaestus was enraged. But unlike the angry nice guy, the nice god was smart enough not to blame her.

> *Just because I am crippled, Zeus's daughter Aphrodite*
> *will always spurn me and love that devastating Ares,*
> *just because of his stunning looks and racer's legs*
> *while I am a weakling, lame from birth, and who's to blame?*
> *Both my parents—who else? If only they'd never bred me!*[18]

Hephaestus knew the bitter truth: women like the strong and spurn the weak. But he also knew that women are not to blame—on a certain level, they just can't help it.

## 2. *Exceptional* Strength

The unequal truth is worse: not only are women's appetites keenly hierarchical, but the hierarchy is steep and unforgiving. Women don't simply like the stronger more, they like only the exceptionally, unusually strong. As for the average men, women find them not simply

---

17 Men are less likely to make this kind of dumb mistake. The naked bodiliness of male appetites is so obvious that men are less oblivious to their fleshy stupidity; therefore, men have less difficulty in identifying the appetite and putting it in its place. Some women might say, "Yeah, he's mean to me and cheats on me, but it's mysterious, magical fate, so I can't leave, etc., etc., etc." But a man will rarely say, "Sure she's mean and cheats on me, but she has such a hot body, so I can't leave"; the men usually know it's just dumb appetite that's talking.

18 Homer, *The Odyssey*, trans. by Robert Fagles (New York: Viking Penguin, 1996), 200.

*less* attractive but wholly *unattractive*.

Consider the average American thirty year old male: He is 5'9 ½ inches tall and just under 200 pounds (so about 30 pounds overweight by the BMI charts);[19] he has a high school diploma, some college but no degree; he has a job and no criminal record; he makes only about $30,000 per year. Sound alluring?

The average American woman does not find such averageness attractive. In fact, women are emphatically disinterested in average.

I was jolted into this realization decades ago while an American student in a European city. In a mixed conversation, some of the guys were celebrating the attractiveness of local girls. I thought the guys were overdoing it, so I decided to inject some balance into the discussion by asking the girls what they thought of the local guys. One girl commented that "I've not seen anyone to make my head turn." The other girls concurred.

I was flabbergasted. What? In an urban area with thousands of young men? Not one of them looked good enough to spark interest?

As the old song goes, young men will stand on the corner and watch "all the girls go by." Yes, *all* of them (of fertile age), pretty much. To be sure, some are far prettier than others, but nearly all are interesting to the male appetite. But their female counterparts will watch "only the *very* exceptional guy go by."

The sharp contrast appears ubiquitous in the supposed free-for-all of the hook-up culture. Young men are routinely disappointed to learn that it's not a free-for-all. A woman can have casual sex almost with anyone she chooses because men don't really discriminate much, but a man must be something special or face repeated rejection.[20] Women, it

---

19  To see a candid display this average guy's physique, see Nickolay Lamm's images that are readily available online.

20  I know an average-looking woman, who spent her twenties as an enthusiastic participant in casual promiscuity sex. She frankly stated, without any obvious pride or shame or other reason for disingenuity, that she needed only a little flirtatious effort to go to bed with any man. Men in the hook-up culture reasonably lament that the world

turns out, are just as sexual as men, but far more discriminating.

The blunt truth is this: *women grade on a pass-fail basis—and most men fail.* Stated otherwise, for women, attraction is like an on/off switch, and few men can flip the switch. In sharp contrast, as we'll elaborate in the next chapter, for men, it's more like a dimmer. The average fertile-aged man finds the vast majority of fertile-aged women attractive, though some more attractive than others. The average woman just does not reciprocate the interest.

How do women distinguish the few from the many? In part by *comparison*. Exceptional strength is often relative. Here and elsewhere, Jane Austen is a reliable guide. Consider the scene where Mr. Knightley, whom Emma had known for years, really catches her eye for the first time:

> There he was, among the standers-by, where he ought not to be; he ought to be dancing, — not classing himself with the husbands, and fathers, and whist-players, who were pretending to feel an interest in the dance till their rubbers were made up, — so young as he looked! He could not have appeared to greater advantage perhaps any where, than where he had placed himself. His tall, firm, upright figure, among the bulky forms and stooping shoulders of the elderly men, was such as Emma felt must draw every body's eyes.[21]

Mr. Knightley "could not have appeared to greater advantage" because he looked so good by *comparison*. His relative superiority made him look very, very good to Emma. She was so pleased that she thought (erroneously) that the whole world must see his allure.

*The Friend Zone is real—and it's really unfriendly.*

There is a remarkable innocence in all this that men often fail to appreciate. Men tend to be far less discriminate and far more generous in their bodily affections. Therefore, men rarely form close friendships with fertile-aged women without feeling some interest, tension, etc. In

---

would be a better place if women were equally as indiscriminate as men. Men like the prettier, but are still generous toward the average. Women are far stingier.

21  Jane Austen, *Emma* (Mineola, NY: Dover Pubs. 2012), 218.

those cases, the decent man knows that he must make a conscious effort to *not* think of the woman in that way. Men thereby consciously create a mental zone in order to manage those relationships; men "friendzone" women.

The same is not true of women, except regarding the exceptional man. For the most part, young women do not need to "friendzone" a man by creating a segregated mental zone. Only the exceptional alpha male requires this treatment. As for all the others, whether beta, gamma or otherwise, Nature has friendzoned them for her.

Yes, nice guys, the Friend Zone exists, and it's not very friendly. But you can't fairly blame the woman.

Still, the innocence of her disinterest makes it all the more painful, doesn't it? It really isn't her fault. You're unattractive because you are weak and feeble. Instead, like Hephaestus, you should instead blame your parents, of Nature, or Fate—they have made you so inadequate that your sexual interest in her provokes not reciprocal affection but only mild irritation or amusement. She's probably too kind to even think it herself, let alone tell you, but I just did.

But before you completely despair, read the next chapter.

## D. What Men Like

Even if men are more generous and inclusive with their affections, they are part of the problem too. In its own ways, the male appetite exhibits a scandalous disregard for equality.

### 1. Fertility

*"...as round above as she was round below."*[22]

Men are at times absurdly predictable. At times, men are so obtuse and single-minded in their appetites that no democratic veil can successfully conceal them.

---

22  Oscar Hammerstein II, *Oklahoma!* (1943).

Male sexual appetite, like female appetite, is at root interested in only one thing—*offspring*—and so it's keenly focused on one female attribute: *fertility*, broadly understood. Remember that sex is by nature for offspring, and that women by nature not only hold all the eggs, but do all the bearing and nursing of children. The male is eagerly looking for women who can bear, nurse, and raise intelligent offspring for him.[23]

This fertility, in a full sense, has five main aspects.

*First and most generally*, men are interested in healthy women of fertile age. Women are fertile, on average, during a roughly thirty year span between 15 and 45, with peak fertility in their early 20s. Among these women, men especially like women who have the thicker, longer hair, good skin, and pretty face (facial proportion and symmetry) that all indicate the health necessary to bear, nurse, and raise offspring.

*Second*, going to the bottom, as it were, men want smart, big-brained, and thus big-headed offspring. They really like women who look like they can bear them. We considered this sometimes-veiled fact in our opening chapter. The curve here has at least three possible connections with intelligent offspring.[24]

*Third*, moving further north, men are interested in *available* fertility. A small waist is a strong indication that the woman is not pregnant. As an added bonus, the tiny waist may even suggest that the woman has never been pregnant; so the man sees that his big-brained child might even enjoy the advantages of primogeniture (first birth).

*Fourth*, continuing our journey up, men are very interested in a woman's apparent ability to nurse those offspring. Men like full

---

23  He thus appears to be rather selfish. But remember he can't help it.

24  This curve may (1) give the illusion of a large pelvis, even if the primary curve is padding; (2) suggest a well-padded (and thus protected) broad pelvis; and, (3) indicate a fat that according to some studies, may produce certain chemicals that aid in prenatal brain development. "The Brain/Butt Theory," *Chicago Tribune*, Nov. 18, 2007; Sophia Borland, "Fat Found in Women's Bottoms Helps to Build Babies' Brains," *Daily Mail*, Jan. 17, 2015.

breasts; for they suggest, or give the illusion of, serious nursing potential (even though the enlarged breast usually consists in fat and not actual milk).[25]

*Fifth*, looking even higher, men are very interested in a woman's apparent patience and kindness—qualities necessary for the survival of those offspring. Young children are enormously labor-intensive, annoying, and burdensome, they are thus highly vulnerable to neglect and even abuse. A man likes a woman who appears to have the smile, patience, and kindness necessary to raise those big-brained, well-nursed kids, and care for them all the way to adulthood, so they, in turn, can reproduce and preserve his own genetic line. Men are eagerly looking for the temperament that anyone would want in hiring a nanny.

Now some of this seems animalistic. But in truth, these appetites reflect some biological facts that distinguish humans from other animals: our intelligence and upright stature. Indeed, female curves (and men's craving for them) distinguish us from the other primates as much as the opposable thumb.[26] Men are animals only because they are *rational* animals.

Although decidedly *humanist*, the male appetite is not *democratic*. It involves some brutal, stark hierarchies. Some women—i.e., those with an hourglass figure and a pleasing disposition—are much more popular with males. A woman without any of the five traits listed above may seem as non-existent to men as the short, poor, timid man is to women.

As Jane Austen candidly noted, despite what men may say, they are not very "philosophic on the subject of beauty," and will readily give their preferences to a woman lacking in intelligence or social standing, simply because she is "pretty and good-natured." Indeed, men actually

---

25 "How fair and how pleasant art thou, O love, for delights! This thy stature is like to a palm tree, and thy breasts to clusters of grapes. I said, I will go up to the palm tree, I will take hold of the boughs thereof: now also thy breasts shall be as clusters of the vine..." Song of Sol. 7:6–8.

26 *See* B.J. Dixon et al., "Female Waist-to-Hip Ratio, Body Mass Index and Sexual Attractiveness in China," 56 *Current Zoology* 175–81 (2010).

"think such beauty, and such temper, the highest claims a woman could possess."[27]

At the risk of undue repetition, let me emphasize that men, like women, have other interests besides appetite. Men will honestly report a conscious attraction to a woman's intelligence, virtue, wealth, achievements, etc. But as with women, men's rational marital desires do not *displace*, but *refine* and *perfect*, the foundational, bodily, subrational appetite. In a similar way, a fine dinner party involves many considerations, but good-tasting food is always the foundation.

Some of the confusion arises because what for one sex is a conscious or rational motive is for the other sex primarily subrational and often unconscious. Strength, especially financial strength, appeals to both the subrational and the rational in women, but only to the rational in men (this is why men grossly overestimate the degree to which women are calculating gold-diggers). Conversely, a pleasant disposition appeals to the subrational and rational in men, but mainly to the rational in women. Another way to approach this is to speak of priorities: both sexes show an interest in, say, confidence or a pleasing physique, but the sexes prioritize these very differently. A wardrobe basic for one sex can often be a mere accessory for the other.

---

27 "You...are unjust to Harriet. Harriet's claims to marry well are not so contemptible as you represent them. She is not a clever girl, but she has better sense than you are aware of, and does not deserve to have her understanding spoken of so slightingly. Waiving that point, however, and supposing her to be, as you describe her, only pretty and good-natured, let me tell you, that in the degree she possesses them, they are not trivial recommendations to the world in general, for she is, in fact, a beautiful girl, and must be thought so by ninety-nine people out of an hundred; and till it appears that men are much more philosophic on the subject of beauty than they are generally supposed; till they do fall in love with well-informed minds instead of handsome faces, a girl, with such loveliness as Harriet, has a certainty of being admired and sought after, of having the power of chusing from among many, consequently a claim to be nice. Her good-nature, too, is not so very slight a claim, comprehending, as it does, real, thorough sweetness of temper and manner, a very humble opinion of herself, and a great readiness to be pleased with other people. I am very much mistaken if your sex in general would not think such beauty, and such temper, the highest claims a woman could possess." Jane Austen, *Emma* (Mineola, NY: Dover Pubs. 2012), 41.

Much could be said of the various ways that male appetite for female fertility involves obnoxious inequalities. But they seem to fall into three categories.

First, women are unequal to other women. Women are *not* equally pretty, shapely, and pleasant. Indeed, half of all women are below average in these respects. Most women do not have an hourglass figure— many enjoy only one of the two popular curves, many have neither. Further, regardless of their initial genetic endowments, many (if not most) lack the wealth, leisure time, and/or determination necessary to preserve their youthful figures into their forties and beyond (that is, to preserve the appearance of available fertility precisely as actual fertility dissipates). Moreover, not all women have the ready smile and easy laughter that men prize. Whether by temperament, harsh personal experience, or otherwise, many women find it very difficult to be cheerful. In some cases, to use the vulgar colloquialism, some women have the "resting b—h face," and some really like to rest their faces. As Kate's aunt cautions her in *A Tree Grows in Brooklyn*: "You don't want to frown like that, Kate. The fellas don't like that at all."[28]

Second, women become inferior to their younger selves. As a woman ages, her attractiveness rises and then falls mercilessly along with her fertility. Women's fertility initially increases into a woman's early twenties, then declines, slowly at first, and then more rapidly in her late thirties, and collapses with menopause. Women experience a contemporaneous, accelerating decline in allure. In their forties, some women feel like their attractiveness to new mates falls off a cliff.[29]

Consider one woman's candid account: "I really wish I'd known that once you're in your late 30s, men are pretty thin on the ground. And once you're in your 40s, it's as though they've been wiped off the face of the Earth. A woman over 45 on an internet dating site is made to feel as welcome as a parking ticket. The sites may be full of single men

---

28 Frank Davis & Tess Slesinger, *A Tree Grows in Brooklyn* (1945) (screenplay adaptation of Betty Smith's novel by the same name (1943)).

29 As we will discuss subsequently, marriage can have a remarkable effect of extending the husband's bodily attraction toward his wife, well past menopause.

in their 40s, but they sure aren't looking to meet women of the same age!"[30]

Third, as this anecdote reveals, women are also unequal to men. While a woman's value declines, a man's stock frequently continues to rise into his thirties and can stay high well past forty. This inequality appears particularly noxious to the smart, successful woman. While she finds that her appeal stagnates and then declines, even if she diligently keeps her waistline, she sees her nerdy male classmate become much more attractive as he develops his career, even as he also develops a paunch. Moreover, while his newfound socio-economic strength is a boon, her comparable success doesn't seem to help at all, and sometimes even hurts.

### 2. *Exclusive* Fertility

The unequal facts get worse when we distinguish men's *marital* or *domestic* appetite from their sexual appetite in general. Whereas a woman's appetite is largely consistent, whether seeking either a hook-up or a husband, a man's unchosen appetite for *domesticated* sex involves obsession with *exclusive* fertility.

To understand this peculiar feature, first recall the ways in which men are radically unequal to women. Men don't bear children but sire them. Consequently, they can produce potentially an unlimited number of offspring but are not quite sure as to their identity. At first glance, the man's best evolutionary course seems to be to pursue quantity over quality—to spread his seed as far and wide and indiscriminately as possible—to have as many offspring as possible and just hope for the best.

But there have long been two major checks on this approach. First, the chances for reproductive success were always low as long as all the other guys were doing the same thing. Second, because women

---

30  Claudia Connell, *The Lonely Account of My Sex and the City Lifestyle*, http://www.dailymail.co.uk/femail/article-2227880/The-lonely-legacy-Sex-And-The-City-lifestyle-Claudia-Connell-gives-painfully-honest-account-came-living-middle-age.html#ixzz3OnT1z2q4

were stuck with the quality strategy, they had an evolutionary interest in inducing men to join them—to attract them to stick around and contribute resources to their joint offspring.[31]

These restraints turned men toward the quality strategy, (a/k/a domesticity). Common sense and all other archaeological evidence indicate that men have lived in households with the mother of their offspring for millions of years. Today the male has a well-developed *appetite* for domesticity—to attach himself to a woman and join her in caring for their joint offspring. Let's call this the Quality Strategy as opposed to the Quantity Strategy.[32] Marital attraction happens when her Quality Strategy marries his Quality Strategy.

But man's hardwired Quality Strategy involved a grave danger. Men never really lost their ability and latent appetite for mass reproduction, and with so many men becoming house-men (the original meaning of hus-band), an evolutionary opportunity arose that the roving alpha male found too sweet to resist: I can get quantity *and* quality, because now the woman has a house-man who's stupid enough to care for all her offspring—including mine! And she will happily participate in my scheme, for she will get the benefit of diversifying her investments in male gametes, all while still enjoying the resources brought by her reliable, dutiful house-man. A win for me, a win for her, and a win for our offspring![33]

But there's one massive loser, of course, the house-man, who unwittingly invests all his resources in the hot guys' offspring. In response to this danger, male appetite, over millions of years, became infused with a primal fear of domesticity with unreliable women. To state it plainly, men have a hardwired, visceral revulsion to the risk of unwittingly serving as nanny to the hot guy's kids. It's evolutionary suicide. Men

---

31 Another major check, at least in the last several hundred years, has been the risk of sexually transmitted infections, but it is unclear whether that danger existed long enough to affect the evolved appetite.

32 This Quality Strategy might involve polygamy or monogamy—the two great rival systems in history.

33 "These were suggestions which human selfishness could not withstand," Federalist No. 15.

don't like it—not at all.

Male inferiority thus infects the male marital appetite with insecurity. The prospect of female infidelity is generally fatal to male domesticity, for the man risks losing not only exclusive access to his partner, but also depleting his own resources to benefit another man's offspring. In such cases, it's far better just to revert to the quantity strategy by spreading his seed around.[34]

The insecurity of the evolved human male gives rise to the (in)famous double standard: chastity is essential to female allure. At a subrational level, women signal their reliability by sexual restraint. A woman's apparent bodily generosity signals unreliability and thus aggravates male insecurity. Consequently, a woman's allure depends on a display of not only bodily fertility, but also bodily stinginess. Male stinginess, in contrast, is less important to male allure.

To be sure, both men and women rightly deplore marital infidelity. At a rational level, adultery equally offends men and women's common sense of justice. The marital promise is sacred and should never be broken.

Even at a subrational level, the threat of a husband's infidelity offends the female appetite. She'd prefer that all his offspring be also her offspring, so that his attention and other resources are directed exclusively at her household. The "other woman" is thus a threat to her offspring.

But an unreliable mate is far more disastrous to male reproductive success and thus almost radioactive to the evolved male appetite. At a fundamental level, the woman does indeed fear the man who will impregnate her and leave; but much more does the man fear the woman who will get pregnant by another man—and stay.

Besides creating a radically unequal double standard, this insecurity subjects women to a brutal two-fold classification system whereby male appetite segregates "quantity" women from "quality" women. Just as

---

34 In our times, the usual response is less adventurous: indifference and retreat via porn and masturbation.

Nature has built for women a Friend Zone, Nature has constructed for men both a "Quantity Zone" and a "Quality Zone. " And once a woman falls into the former, she is usually ineligible for the latter.[35] To speak very bluntly, men, by nature, deem a slut to be unmarriageable.

But it's not men's fault. Just as women don't deliberately friendzone a man, men don't deliberately "Quantity Zone" a woman—Nature does it for them.

Escape from the male Quantity Zone can be far more daunting than escape from the female Friend Zone. Helen Gurley Brown famous pulled off this gymnastic trick: she bounced from bed to bed throughout her twenties and early thirties, eventually using the promiscuity bed as a springboard to land into the marriage bed with a wealthy man. She then advised other women to do the same via her book, *Sex and the Single Girl* and her magazine *Cosmopolitan*. Yet both the book and magazine should have come with this warning: "results atypical—really, really atypical."[36]

Nor is the male primordial fear of infidelity adequately allayed by modern sterilization and DNA-testing. It bears repeating that the million-year-old appetite for sex, like that for food, doesn't care about modern technology. The subrational doesn't get the message.[37] Our appetites read smoke signals, not email. Male appetite still relies on the million-year old signal for reassurance: female chastity and modesty.

---

35 "A man fishes for two reasons: he's either sport fishing or fishing to eat, which means he's either going to try to catch the biggest fish he can, take a picture of it, admire it with his buddies and toss it back to sea, or he's going to take that fish on home, scale it, fillet it, toss it in some cornmeal, fry it up, and put it on his plate. This, I think, is a great analogy for how men seek out women." Steve Harvey, *Act Like a Lady, Think Like a Man: What Men Really Think About Love, Relationships, Intimacy, and Commitment* (New York: Amistad Pubs. 2010), 70.

36 I have heard of a woman who, in her words, also went "from ho to housewife." But she reports that the transition was quite difficult. For her part, Mrs. Brown explained that she never divulged the details of her many "frisky" sexcapades to her husband: somehow she knew he wouldn't like to know.

37 Anyone on a diet knows the appetite's stubborn fears—e.g., it keeps thinking a famine is coming. Male appetite is no different.

The evidence for modern men's strong interest in this ancient reassurance appears ubiquitous. For instance, many women may fantasize about winning and domesticating a famous womanizer, but men do not dream of marrying prostitutes.[38] Similarly, once married, some women will acquiesce, very reluctantly, in sharing a husband, especially if he's quite wealthy, but almost no men have the stomach for such generosity. Men are just not very generous or open-minded about it: men won't share.

Some of this evidence is in unexpected places. So strong is this fear that it influences even the undomesticated male appetite—the inclination to hook-ups, porn, etc. Even when men are consciously shunning quality sexuality in favor of "quantity" sexuality, they exhibit a strong preference for not only the youthful and fertile, but also the (relatively) inexperienced. Here again, the market is brutally honest. Anyone passingly familiar with pornography—that is, anyone who's ever walked by a newsstand in a major city or seen the list of films available for purchase in a hotel room—knows that a most common subject is a young woman whose sexual experience is almost as limited as her sexual appetite is unlimited (e.g., barely legal, etc.). Conversely, you'd search in vain for a title like "Crystal's Retirement Party" or "Jasmin's 400th time."[39]

Or consider the peculiar market for prostitutes: experience here generally has a negative value. A "help wanted" advertisement would read, "No experience necessary—or desired." A reasonably pretty woman may auction off her virginity for millions of dollars, but she will receive far less for her 100th customer.

---

38 The movie "Pretty Woman" must be one of the greatest democratic frauds ever perpetrated against women's martial aspirations. In the film, a very wealthy and obscenely handsome man woos and marries a prostitute of merely attainable beauty and mediocre disposition. The film told women in our age what many desperately wanted to hear, but that no man, even today, could say with a straight face. No man fantasizes about marrying such a woman—and no rich handsome man goes bride hunting in the brothel.

39 Consider also, among many other examples, the stripper. Her initial clothing is very much an essential part of the allure.

Another place to look is in the candid vulgarity of young men. Such men tend to declare their appetites for "hot girls" with a guileless innocence—without ideological filter or democratic pretension, especially when they speak anonymously. They speak loud and clear that a woman's hotness is significantly impaired by excessive generosity. To be sure, young men like youthful, very fertile looking women, and they like women who seem eager to put that fertility to use. But too much actual use, and such women can become rapidly un-hot. Consider the fate of Miley Cyrus. When she burst on the scene, casting off Hannah Montana and the bonds of sexual innocence, she was enormously popular. Readers of *Maxim* magazine voted her the hottest woman alive. But just a year later, after a single vulgar display at the American Music Awards ceremony, her ranking plummeted to #25. What about her had changed? Not the shape of her body, but her excessive generosity with it.

More on point, *Maxim* once asked its readers to rank the "unsexiest" women. The top five women all had two distinctive characteristics: (1) they were all female celebrities and thus had unusually attractive faces and figures, but (2) they all had acquired a public reputation for an unusual degree of promiscuity or vulgarity.

## E. Our Veils, Mutual Deceptions, and Self-Deceptions

*Maxim*'s one-time poll was highly controversial—an understandably so. The poll tore off one of our most precious veils. Of all of the hard truths listed in this chapter, none is today more fiercely veiled or angrily denied than the role that female chastity plays in the male sexual appetite, and especially the marital appetite. Even the editors of *Maxim* put the veil back on, and implausibly explained their rankings solely in terms of the women's appearance (all of whom were far above average) rather than their apparent promiscuity.

In fact, there are probably three veils at work here, only one of which is egalitarian. One veil is probably universal, present in all societies, no matter how undemocratic. Recall that the fundamental basis of male allure is strength. As such, the natural fact of male insecurity is unpleasant to both aspiring attractive men and to women who like them. A man's timidity makes him un-hot. Accordingly, both sexes are disinclined to reflect on male insecurity and are more comfortable thinking of a woman's derivative and secondary insecurity: her need to reassure the male appetite by preserving the appearance of reserve or modesty. Indeed, the insecurity is so deep in men that it is largely unconscious, whereas women's derivative insecurity is far more conscious. So in the famous song, we hear of the girl—clothed only in an itsy-bitsy bikini—who was afraid to come out of the water. But the primary and deeper fear belonged to her potential husband, even if he didn't feel nervous at all.

This first veil explains why the old wives—who are usually reliable guides in these matters—only got this truth half right. They warned that a man would not "buy the cow if he could get the milk for free." But that's not quite it. Free samples aren't the problem, and the man doesn't care if the woman is a chump. Rather, the real motivator is his primal fear that *he* will be the chump: the guy who purchases and cares for the cow, while lots of other guys still get the milk for free.

To women, this may seem strange. Men seem to have big egos—especially the very swashbuckling man that women prize. Such a man, women think, will not be insecure, but just say to himself, "Of course she gave me the free sample because I am just so awesome, but she won't give it to the others who are so clearly not as awesome." Indeed, he might really say that to himself, but the male appetite is far less stupid. Millions of years of evolution have taught humility: lots of other equally charming fellows will always be around to successfully get the free sample—and leave him with their offspring to raise.

A second veil arises from a sort of natural prudence. The male fear of cuckoldry, if unveiled, provokes feelings and expressions of jealousy. But distrust breeds distrust, and is thus fatal to the mutual affection of spouses. Contemplating the prospect of adultery is disastrous. Prudence, then, dictates that a veil be placed over this fear.

A third veil arises from our democratic passions. It seems far preferable to pretend that sexual freedom promotes gender equality, where everybody plays and everybody wins. Women dislike the double standard, and of course, the women who've eagerly jumped into the modern free-for-all don't want to be counted as sluts—or still worse, fools.[40]

It's also highly problematic for men. They are often the fiercest deniers because to state the truth plainly is to reveal how much contemporary sexual freedom involves men and women engaging in an exploitative inequality that harms women more. In pornography, prostitution, and promiscuity, women's bodies become commodities consumed by men. The more women do what the men want them to do, the less the men like them. The results are disastrous for the woman with the slightest marital aspirations. Men don't want women to know this. And men, who are (like women) frequently self-centered but rarely malicious, don't want to know it themselves.

This veil over the male appetite for female chastity has something of an analogue to the veil covering the female appetite for male strength. This latter desire is so outrageously aristocratic that it offends our democratic sensibilities. The aristocratic fact is unpleasant to most men, as most men are actually average or worse (i.e., losers). And it's unpleasant to democratic women, for they do not like to think of themselves as sexual elitists. So both sexes prefer the veil.

Here too there can be a kind of dishonest, exploitative relationship between women and men—where men become less attractive to women precisely insofar as they comply with women's demands. A servile, overly-compliant boyfriend is like the sexually adventurous girlfriend, and suffers a comparable fate. Women, no less than men, are willful and want their own way. Therefore, the woman wants her partner to comply with her wishes. But at some point, the more the man does precisely what the woman demands, the less she likes him—because her appetite craves male strength, not servility.

---

40 As we know, it's not a free for all for men either. Alpha males regularly get the invitations, while most men are politely or impolitely told that their presence is unnecessary and unwelcome.

In the whole male-female area, then, equality has become the enemy of not only candor but also kindness. Behind all the democratic veils, the sexes can become mired in mutual deception and mutual degradation.

But let me end this unpleasant chapter on a less negative note. There is some innocence even here. This mutual deception ordinarily is not mutual deceit. For the most part, men and women don't lie to one another. Malice is not the usual culprit, even where a woman nags her boyfriend into servility, or a man pressures his girlfriend into sexual "open-mindedness." Rather, each sex typically deceives itself as much as it deceives the other.

# CHAPTER FIVE

## WHAT WE'VE FORGOTTEN: NATURE'S STUBBORN HOPEFUL FACTS

*Kindness and truth shall meet...*

Our democratic veils hide some stubborn hard facts. Women crave strength, especially excellence. Men crave both fertility and the reassurance of exclusivity (chastity). In none of these respects is Nature a democracy. Nor is Nature a meritocracy: most people, including the most earnest and kind, seem stuck with sexual mediocrity and inferiority. But as we'll see in this chapter, our democratic veils also conceal some very hopeful facts.

Perhaps the most fundamental question in philosophy and religion is man's relationship with nature. Much has been thought, said, and written about whether nature is kind, malicious, or indifferent to humanity. Ancient philosophers like Aristotle tended to emphasize nature's benevolence, while modern philosophers, like Hobbes and Freud, focused on nature's indifference, if not hostility.

In the area of marital enterprise, I think the ancients were basically right, up to a point. While Nature is not a perfectly beneficent mother, she is most certainly not a malicious b—h. Nature is more like an aunt who is kind, absent-minded, and occasionally testy. If you work and play with her, she will usually be quite generous (though sometimes she forgets), but when you ignore her, she gets real mean. She's even worse when you try to shove her aside. As the Latin poet said, "if you drive away Nature with a pitchfork, she'll come back with a vengeance."[1]

As we have seen, Aunt Nature is not a democrat and won't comply with our egalitarian demands. And she's reacted very badly to all our denial and anger, all our veils, mutual deceptions, and self-deceptions.

But for the man or woman who is looking for an enduring loving relationship (maybe even marriage), Aunt Nature actually still has a lot to offer to her attentive nephews and nieces. She doesn't demand slavish devotion, just some time and attention.

Therefore, let's sit at her feet and listen to Aunt Nature, and consider the following seven hopeful facts with the same candor with which we looked at the hard ones. This chapter should be much more pleasant to the marriage minded.

### 1. Men and women are from the same planet—Earth.

Our web of veils, deceptions, and self-deceptions often lead one sex to view the other as alien. As a young single man, when hearing the title of John Gray's famous book, *Men are from Mars, Women are from Venus*, I said to myself, "That's not true. Men are from Earth. Women are not." Many women have said the converse.

Gray was wrong. And I was wrong. Women and men are both from the same planet: Earth. We belong to the same two-sexed terrestrial species, and all of us result from countless generations of male-female unions. Every man is as much a son to his mother as to his father; every woman is as much a daughter to her father as to her mother. Our common human nature, including our reciprocal sexuality, evolved together on this Earth. We are, up to a point,[2] made for this earth and made for each other. This is the insight of many religious traditions.[3]

---

1    *Naturam expellas furca, tamen usque recurret.* Horace, *Epistles*, 1.10.24.

2    Only up to a point; of course, we don't seem to ever be fully, perfectly happy here, and life here is often burdensome, and tragic, sometimes gruesomely so. These are facts too.

3    "God has made for you your mates of your own nature." Quran 16:42. "Therefore people (still) are not happy when alone. He desired a mate. He became as

At times, this insight can be cause for great joy. Charlie Brown was in love with the Little Redhaired Girl. When he found her pencil with teeth marks on it, he was all the more enthralled: "She nibbles her pencil, she's human!" Anyone who's ever been infatuated knows what a joy such knowledge can be.[4] The most exquisite man or woman you ever will know is not an alien or a god, neither extraterrestrial nor divine—but a human being. She nibbles her pencil, like me. He spills his coffee, like me. And so on.

Moreover, the sexes share in common not only some lovable foibles but also many appetites—even if in different proportions. Almost none of the features that one sex likes in another will be exclusive to one: consequently, both women and men like to excel in competition, both men and women can be self-conscious about their appearance.

But there will be differences in proportion and priority. So, to cite one important example, both sexes like smiles and confidence, but smiling is more important to a woman's beauty, and confidence to a man's. A smile is a woman's staple but a man's accessory; confidence is a man's basic but a woman's accessory.

The sexes likewise share many common interests, even if in different proportions. Here too, this co-naturality is such a joy to our affections. That's why a feminine woman's interest in sports can be so pleasing to a man, or a masculine man's interest in a book club can be so appealing to a woman. After all, by nature we are inclined to the household, and thus to enjoy things in common besides the sex act. We take delight in the prospect of such shared joys.

The problem in our time is that these facts give our egalitarian passions a false hope. Men and women share so much in common that full

---

big as man and wife embracing each other. He parted this very body into two. From that came husband and wife. Therefore, said Yajnavalkya, this (body) is one-half of oneself, like one of the two halves of a split pea. Therefore this space is indeed filled by the wife. He was united with her." Brihadaranyaka Upanishad 1.4. 3. "This is now bone of my bones, and flesh of my flesh." Gen. 2:23.

4    "*Homo sum, humani nihil a me alienum puto*" [I am a man, nothing human is alien to me]. —Terence. *Etiam viri et feminae* [Even men and women]!—Upham.

equality seems just over the next hill, and all we need to get there is just a bit more effort. But we never get there. When we find we can't stamp out the remaining inequalities, the result is anger—at the other sex, society, or our own sorry selves.

Still, despite our stubborn differences, there is this good news: we are not aliens. Still less are men and women natural enemies. To adapt Lincoln's words: "We are not enemies, but friends. We must not be enemies. Though [egalitarian] passion may have strained, it must not break our bonds of affection."[5]

### 2. You were bred to bond.

Every human being on the Earth has been bred to bond and breed. Even if you don't consciously want to breed, you have been bred to successfully engage in the male-female bond. You are the result of an unbroken succession of successful bonders and breeders. Your matrilineal line, from your mother, back to your maternal grandmother, and beyond, for millions of years, saw nothing but success. And your patrilineal line likewise exhibits ancient, unbroken, consistent fertility. Three things have united *all* your ancestors since the dawn of humanity, whether male or female: they were all human beings, they all survived to adulthood, and they all successfully formed at least one male-female bond that resulted in an adult offspring.

Furthermore, if you could trace your family tree, you'd find that the vast majority of the male-female bonds that made you involved not only a peaceful conception, but an enduring relationship—usually till death did they part. In this sense, the vast majority of your ancestors, both male and female, got and stayed married. Therefore, it is *highly* likely (though not guaranteed—Aunt Nature forgets sometimes) that you have the wherewithal to do the same.

### 3. Double the pleasure, double the fun

Because men and women have been on earth attracting one another as mates for so many thousands of generations, it is highly likely that we

---

5    Abraham Lincoln, "First Inaugural Address" (1861).

not only have the stuff to please the opposite sex, but have developed a pleasure in the pleasing. That is to say, we like to do, for its own sake, what the other sex likes us to do.

As a general rule, both men and women fantasize not only about a pleasing mate, but about *pleasing* that pleasing mate. Women's fantasies are filled with very attractive men who are filled with desire for the female protagonist. Male desires are similar. Rarely does anyone fantasize about mating with someone wholly indifferent, contemptuous, asleep, or basically dead. Indeed, often the fantasy involves our counterpart's *greater* pleasure.

Moreover, men and women seem hardwired, to a certain extent, to like doing those things that happen to make them look attractive. Consider, for instance, male hierarchical competitiveness. As we noted, women like the man who projects relative strength—strength especially relative to those around him. Women like winners. Men, over time, developed a pleasure in competition, in competing in hierarchies and winning.[6] Men thus like to engage in mating displays—and are usually unconscious of the effect.

So much do men enjoy competition that they have developed a vicarious pleasure in watching other men compete—even more than the women who are the primal reason for the contest. Men typically like watching sports more than women. Men like looking at the quarterback striving to finish the game-winning drive; women like this too, but usually less so.

A similarly derivative, but powerful pleasure attends female beauty. In general, men take pleasure in female prettiness (duh). In general, women take a derivative pleasure in looking pretty. Like the male

---

6 This competition has an adversarial aspect to it, but keep in mind, the winners have a vested interest in not utterly alienating the losers, in part because men are social animals and are more likely to survive, but also because without the beta males, the alpha males don't look alpha. So men have an appetite not only compete in hierarchies, but also to show magnanimity and fellowship with the losers. In this limited but interesting respect, men have an appetite for comradeship that women competing for mates do not have.

display of strength, the female display of fertility typically does not involve any conscious intent to mate. Thus, it is often said with reason that women dress for themselves, or for other women, and not for men.

Women's pleasure in looking pretty struck me one day in Dallas where I was on public transportation during the annual Mary Kay convention. A whole throng of women entered the car. They were generally middle aged, married, and dressed to the nines. They looked very nice. Still, I suspect that very few, if any, were looking to attract an adulterous liaison. They just liked looking pretty. Most women, on average and in general, take some pleasure in looking pretty.[7]

Similarly, like the male taste for vicarious competition, there's a female taste for vicarious beauty. Consider the realm of women's magazines and beauty pageants. Such magazines and pageants tend to be filled with very good-looking women—that is, healthy, fertile-looking women. Although male appetite is the ultimate cause of such display, on average and in general, men get bored of watching beauty pageants, fashion shows, etc. (even much quicker than women get bored of sports). In this respect, women like looking at good-looking women more than men do.

Of course, it bears repeating that these secondary, complementary pleasures are no more perfectly universal than the primary appetites we reviewed in the prior chapter. Indeed, lots of men dislike sports, and lots of women are indifferent to fashion shows. And more importantly, the whole matter is fraught with asymmetry and disproportion. To cite one bemusing example, men are generally flummoxed by the degree to which women take an interest in certain adornments like shoes and manicures. Women's desire for pretty hands and cute shoes is typically far greater than any male interest in them.

So, all this said, it's highly likely that you have the wherewithal to please a potential spouse, and that this pleasing can be somewhat pleasant and not a terrible chore. After all, you were bred to do this thing.

---

7    I'll go further. I believe that women take pleasure in some level of modesty, reserve, etc. Indeed, I suspect that most women view some limited modesty to be an utter precondition to feeling "sexy."

## 4. Men grade women on a very generous curve.

*"When I'm not near the girl I love...I love the girl I'm near."*[8]

So you learned the truth, whether at seventeen or just seventeen minutes ago, that men like beauty queens, with all their youthful fertility and youthful inexperience. For many women this news does not appear to be very good. In fact, it seems downright infuriating or depressing.

In both respects, however, male appetite is far, far more generous to women than women suppose. The error arises in this way. The female appetite, as we have noted, is aristocratic and thus likes the few and spurns the many. A genuinely average man is simply unattractive. Women generally have some awareness of their own brutal selectivity, despite our democratic veils. Women are also well aware that men are peculiarly interested in beauty, and most women have at least a vague sense that men like chastity too.

At the next step, however, women's democratic prejudices take over. They assume that male appetite grades women's beauty and chastity according to the same kind of onerous pass/fail exam by which female appetite judges male strength.

Many women reach this step, I believe, and can't move forward. Not surprisingly, they remain stuck on denial, anger or depression.

What's needed, however, is to toss off another democratic veil. Men and women are not equal here: the male appetite grades both female beauty and female chastity on a very generous curve. Men are more welcoming and inclusive in this respect.

Let's consider, for instance, the average female figure. Men like average—they really do. As an old married man, candor here would be unbecoming, so I'll let a wise middle-aged woman set you straight: "The average American woman is a sexy, sumptuous 5'4", 143-pound groove-thing with a 39-inch built-in seat cushion. She's got nerve in her curves and would never consider using a Cheerio for a lifesaver. She's

---

8  E.Y. Harburg, *Finian's Rainbow* (1947).

also got what the average American man is dying to get his hands on. That's real."[9] In other words, the average woman's figure (provided she appears to be still close to fertile age) is a *delight* to most men.

To be sure, men have *preferences*, but the preferences are not *prerequisites*. The vast majority of women are already "in the house." The male appetite does indeed grade women, but it's not a 1-10 scale, with half of women at 5 or below. Rather, it's a 0-100 scale, with the vast majority of women already at an 80. If a woman looks like she can bear healthy children and appears neither so thin nor so fat that she *appears* likely to die within a decade, the male appetite will register its decided enthusiastic approval.

In this way, the male appetite is a dimmer switch, even as the female appetite is a simple on/off switch. It doesn't take much to turn men on.

Why is the male appetite so generous and inclusive? Remember that Nature has put all of humanity's eggs in one basket—the bodies of fertile-aged women who can only have a few offspring. Such bodies are precious to the species and consequently precious to the male appetite. Men can have thousands of offspring: they thus have reason to be more welcoming and more generous with their bodies.

Here too, the evidence for this inequality and misunderstanding appears everywhere. Women complain of countless bodily imperfections: the muffin top, cellulite, the imperfect nose, *ad infinitum*, and think of themselves as inadequate or even ugly. In our times, countless young women, hoping for relationships or even marriage, have looked at themselves in the mirror in comparison with the fitness models, and understandably thought to themselves, "my boyfriend or husband is going to be disgusted with me."

If you are such a woman, let me say the following: No, no, no, no, and no. I was going to scream at you, but that would be ungentlemanly. Yes, the fitness model is more appealing than you, and no, her superiority has little to do with airbrushing (sorry—forget that pleasing myth). But

---

9    Deborah Arneson, *Fries, Thighs, and Lies: The Girlfriend's Guide to Getting the Skinny on Fat* (Laguna Beach, CA: Basic Health Publications, 2007), 2.

the following is also true: if you appear to be of fertile age and you are within the very, very broad range of average, the bulk of young men already like the way you look and will be very happy to see you disrobed. If you don't believe me, ask for a candid answer from a young man you trust. Better yet: turn to the seemingly happy old wives, whether skinny or fat: look at photos from their fertile days, and ask them for a candid answer as to whether you, with all your alleged imperfections, will be pleasing to a man.

Lacking the experience of the old wives, many intelligent women do not understand the generosity of male appetite: Consider these remarks by the eminently talented, very witty, and very pretty Tina Fey:

> [Thanks to JLo and Beyoncé] a back porch and thick muscular legs were now widely admired. And from that day forward, women embraced their diversity and realized that all shapes and sizes are beautiful.
>
> Ah ha ha. No. I'm totally messing with you. All Beyoncé and JLo have done is add to the laundry list of attributes women must have to qualify as beautiful. Now every girl is expected to have Caucasian blue eyes, full Spanish lips, a classic button nose, hairless Asian skin with a California tan, a Jamaican dance hall ass, long Swedish legs, small Japanese feet, the abs of a lesbian gym owner, the hips of a nine-year-old boy, the arms of Michelle Obama, and doll tits. The person closest to actually achieving this look is Kim Kardashian, who, as we know, was made by Russian scientists to sabotage our athletes.[10]

Very funny, but only true in Hollywood. For the male appetite, all those features might be nice (except the decidedly unfertile hips), but none are absolute prerequisites. In this respect, male appetite *largely* concurs with Coco Chanel: "There are no ugly women in the world, only lazy ones." In fact, male appetite goes further—the average woman of fertile age almost has to *try* to be ugly. I'm serious.

A similar gap between male appetite and female expectation occurs in the area of chastity. Here too, the democratic myth might be the culprit, whereby women project a steep, unforgiving hierarchy onto men. A

---

10  Tina Fey, *Bossypants* (New York: Reagan Arthur, 2011), 22–23.

woman might conclude that unless she is a virgin, she must be a slut in men's eyes. The average woman today, by her twenties, is no longer a virgin, so....

But the male appetite doesn't think like that. Even with his preferences, his appetite is on a dimmer and not that cruel switch.

According to the Center for Disease Control, the median woman between the ages of 25 and 45 has had 4 sexual partners in her lifetime. Around this median, there is significant variation, of course, but the vast majority of women have former partners numbering in the single digits. The most marriage-minded women, on average and in general, are more likely to be somewhat lower on the scale, I suspect.

Do such numbers make the average woman unattractive to the average man? I don't think so. Now I don't know of any good data in this regard. Male appetite for chastity, unlike for fertility, is harder to gauge, in part because it's hard to disentangle it from the other factors that would induce a man to prefer a low number, even a zero. One conscious, rational reason is the fear of bedroom competition with other men in the woman's memory—and the resulting "performance anxiety."[11] Further, some men, for a variety of ethical or religious reasons, might prefer a virgin.[12]

Still, I think it's fair to say that at the level of appetite, men generally impose no strict virginity test. The average American woman's sexual history may somewhat impair, but does not destroy her marital allure. Remember: what male marital appetite is looking for is not some sort of ethical purity but reassurance against the danger of future infidelity.

Further, a woman's history becomes increasingly less problematic as that experience becomes more distant in time. Male appetite does not have an acute memory. Last month's boyfriend is more irksome to men's natural insecurity that a few hook-ups a decade ago.

---

11 According to some reports, erectile dysfunction, arising from performance anxiety, is increasingly common in young men.

12 It would be an interesting question to identify the precise relation between the natural appetite for chastity and the religious or ethical value of chastity.

Conversely, however, as with women's appearance, the generosity of male appetite has limits. Twenty extra pounds is one thing, two hundred extra pounds is something else. Similarly, two former sex partners is one thing, twenty is something else. In both cases, the extreme does indeed gravely impair one's allure. Just as it is foolish for a marriage-minded woman to say, "well, I've gained twenty pounds, I might as well gain two hundred," it is utter folly for her to say, "well, I've already had two sex partners, let's jack that number up to an even twenty." But even here, time can have significant restorative effect.

I should add here that motherhood by another man has a very similar role in impairing, but not destroying, male interest, both on an appetitive and rational level. It's deceitful pandering to insist that single motherhood in no way affects a woman's marital appeal—it does. It's equally false to say that single motherhood utterly destroys that appeal. Single mothers can and do attract good husbands.

Now many men are coy about this "generosity" in their appetites. Some men fear that women are scandalized by the diffusive promiscuity of the male eye. But I think candor is necessary here, for in our times the greater problem is the scandal of women's stupid conclusion that men find them disgusting. Further, the scandal of male generosity, I think, can be mitigated by this additional information: the male appetite may be always "on," but it's easily distracted. A young man may notice, on the level of appetite, *hundreds* of fertile-looking women in the day— maybe thousands if he's in a busy place, but he is likely to forget each one almost immediately. Indeed, without his appetite's attention deficit disorder (ADD), men would have died of lust long ago.

Men often *appear* to contradict my claim here by blunt categorization of women into "hot" and "not." But for the most part, such men are telling only a half truth; they are registering their strong preference in misleading binary language.[13]

---

13 Some men, however, are dishonest jerks, engaging in malicious, egalitarian payback. They know that women have a brutal on/off switch. The men know they have often failed the female pass/fail test. In bitter response, they proclaim women are equally subject to such a test. These bitter men forget that women can't help it, and

In sum, for the most part, men are indeed keenly interested in both youthful fertility and a woman's stinginess in sharing it ("chastity"). But men are equally hard-wired to like the average woman's fertility and chastity, provided she appears to be of fertile age. If you are a marriage-minded woman of that age, it is highly likely that <u>men already like you</u>.

### 5. Women offer a wide diversity of pass/fail tests.

Though the average man likes the average woman, the average woman does not reciprocate. The news appears bad for the average man. It's not great for the average marriage-minded woman either. The woman will observe that there appear to be so many good women and too few "good men" to go around. If heard by the man, the woman's lament, in turn, further enrages him: she's a snob (or worse). And this exchange only further exacerbates the mutual animosity of the sexes.

But there are other considerations. Instead of anger, our democratic man needs to remember another way that women are unequal to men. True, unlike the gentle path to the male appetite, the way to a woman's affections is a steep climb. But women differ from men in one other, happy respect. The path to a man's affection is pretty singular—because fertility is a rather singular concept. But *strength*, the object of women's desires, is multiform. Consequently, there are many paths up to women's affections, because there are many kinds of strength.

The diversity of paths is a boon to the average man because the average man, on average, will not be average in all respects, but be strong in one or more. The ordinary man is thus extraordinary. To be sure very few men will be Mr. Darcy—with three exceptional strengths of height, confidence and wealth, but most men can find some hierarchy in which to compete and display some strength.

Stated otherwise, although women subject men to an onerous pass/fail test, there are many different tests to take, and in large measure, most men can pass at least one of them. Indeed, the prudent man can choose which test to take. To a certain extent, men even get to write the test

that, as I'll elaborate in the next section, the average man can indeed pass the female test.

themselves.

The key for the marriage-minded man is to identify his own strengths, develop new ones, and learn how to display those strengths before single and otherwise marriageable women. We'll elaborate this happy truth in the next chapter.

### 6. The way is broad—greased tightrope not included.

Both men and women complain about mutually conflicting standards. They say the demands of the opposite sex push them into a nearly impossible position: between a rock and a hard place, damned regardless of what they choose. Women perceive that men are interested in both sexuality and reliability—and complain that if they are too sexual they are "sluts," and if they are too reserved they are "prudes." Men, in turn, know that women complain loudly about men's cockiness, but observe that aggressive jerks seem to regularly have pretty girlfriends—so women complain about jerks and reject the nice guys. In either case, the opposite sex seems to put them on a high-wire act—walking across a greased tightrope.

Men and women greatly misunderstand each other. There's no tightrope, let alone a greased one. The path, in both cases, is very broad, with a great deal of room for error. Moreover, as we've already suggested and will discuss below, male kindness and strength, one the one hand, and female chastity and sensuality, on the other, are not opposite but can be largely *complementary*.

### 7. You are a free and rational animal.

As I have repeatedly insisted, human beings have stubborn, hardwired, subrational appetites. But we are more than mere animals: we are also rational and free. Nature has given us appetites but also reason and free will.

Indeed, we will never understand the human sexual appetite if we forget that its chief purpose is the reproduction of free, rational animals. This fact, as we have seen, explains what makes for an especially attractive woman or man: on the one hand, the body to bear and nurse the intelligent child and the pleasant disposition to raise them; on the other hand, the resources to contribute to that enormously labor-intensive enterprise.

We are, then, both bodies and minds—a composite of the two. And by nature the mind is the governor.

Here are some serviceable metaphors. Nature has built the car and the road, but you are still in the driver's seat. Nature has given your guests their appetites, but you get to plan the dinner party. Or, in your dance with Nature, the steps are largely defined, but you get to take the lead, with some room for playful improvisation.

Given the generosity of Aunt Nature, including her provision of intelligence and freedom, it is *highly* likely that you can be successful in the marital enterprise. But so many young people don't know this, especially our most educated, who presume that professional success is easier than marital success. Consider Professor Rachel Lu's observations:

> Today's undergraduates are not, for the most part, radicals and revolutionaries. They harbor conventional hopes of professional success and happy marriages. But while they believe that the first can reliably be secured through hard work and dedication, marriage seems in their minds to require a mysterious mixture of good fortune and good chemistry, perhaps combined with the social status that they hope to win through professional success.

> Unfortunately, they have things exactly backwards. A good marriage is the sort of thing that almost anyone can aspire to, regardless of skills, education, or status. The most important ingredients for marital success are within any individual's power to attain. Professional success, by contrast, does reflect hard work and commitment, but it also depends on complex external factors that no individual person can control.[14]

Nature's not perfect, but she's a lot cuter and kinder than the Market. Dance with her. In the next chapter, I'll show you the main steps.

---

14  Rachel Lu, *Millennials and Marriage*, Public Discourse (Sept. 18, 2013).

### 8. Strong and enduring mutual affection is possible.

This chapter's good news may induce a sad reflection. The very flexibility of male and female appetite that can encourage might also dishearten. The marriage-minded want more than mutual attraction. They want enduring love: they desire that this mutual attraction involve mutual primacy and mutual permanence. That is, they want a relationship where the spouses both cherish one another as their first loves and do so for a long time, even for life. But the very ease with which mutual attraction is possible may suggest that it is also fleeting. She will turn her affections to the stronger, more successful man who comes along; he will lose interest as she ages and her fertility declines.

This desire for such primary and permanent love is natural.[15] The reproduction of free, rational, and fertile adult offspring requires much more work than copulation and pregnancy. To take newborn humans and turn them into adults is enormously labor-intensive and expensive. And the work may last a lifetime if it includes the natural desire to engage in the grandparenting enterprise.[16] Therefore, our sexual desires are naturally infused with longings that point beyond sex, beyond pregnancy, and beyond infancy. As we've discussed—the orientation toward raising and educating children is why women seek males with strength (resources) and men seek females with patient, kind dispositions. For the same reason, both sexes want their affections to be reciprocal, strong, and enduring. It's gonna be a tough road ahead, so let's stick together.

But Aunt Nature has been generous here as well (although in her typically imperfect, absent-minded way). Human beings, on average and in general, have a variety of inclinations that can be very favorable toward enduring, strong marital love. As with sexual attraction, however, the successful reliance on these inclinations requires humble attention and some work.

The first inclination is toward the free focus of the mind. If you actually

---

15  Of course, this desire for enduring love may suggest that human beings have some transcendent, even supernatural orientation.

16  By evolution, man naturally lives in clans, not simple nuclear families.

look around, you'll see that the whole world is full of so much good, beautiful, and other interesting things. Among these beautiful things are very attractive men and women. The more you look, the more you will see this bounty. But our minds, and thus our hearts, cannot see the whole, and must prioritize, and focus on this or that in particular. We can, if we wish, freely choose to turn our attention to this or that good and beautiful thing, this or that beautiful person, or this or that beautiful aspect of that person. By freely doing so, our mind, in turn, orients the heart. By *choosing* to make something primary in our minds it becomes primary in our hearts. Falling in love can largely be a matter of choice.[17]

The second inclination is toward habit. We tend to do what we have repeatedly done. The heart, as well as the body, moves in part by habit. The more we love, the more easily we love. Habits usually require deliberate conscious effort to initiate and maintain. And initiation is harder than maintenance. Consider the habit of regular physical exercise. And of course, some habits are easier to develop than others.

The third inclination is toward love of one's own. Perhaps it may seem a sober fact, but people tend to like more what they can claim as their own. We are more attached to our house than to our apartment, and more attached to our apartment than to our hotel room. What's true of property is also true of people. We love our own things, even where that *ownership* arises from convention and not nature. What becomes our "own" occurs in at least three ways. One is by being a part of ourselves, like our body or mind. A second way is by conventional designation—what our society ratifies as our own. A third way is by our investment of ourselves in something; so, the more we put into something, the more we are loyal to it.[18]

17 For one fascinating study of this, see Mandy Len Catron, "To Fall in Love With Anyone, Do This," *N.Y. Times* (Feb. 13, 2005). My advice: do this *only after* you have good reason to believe that you should fall in love with this person because you believe that in spending a life with him or her, you will become more the man or woman you wish to be.

18 These three ways all serve to bind parents to children. Biological parents have a primordial attachment because offspring are the fruits of their bodies. Conventional designation supplements men's inferiority here—their insecurity as to the identity of

The fourth inclination is toward the love of affection, esteem, or honor. We very much like to be liked by others, especially friends. We want people to think well of us. And we will be inclined to act to win and keep the esteem and affection of others. The choice of friends, therefore, can be of momentous importance as to what kind of men and women we will be.

These four inclinations can provide powerful tools for the establishment of a strong and enduring mutual affection in marriage. First, from the beginning, wives and husbands can take advantage of the inclinations toward focus and habit by making a habit of focusing on their spouses' qualities. A husband should make the regular choice of noticing his wife's beauty; the wife should reciprocate.

Conversely, of course, the spouses should resolve to avoid focusing on one another's faults or other displeasing features. It is not mere *familiarity* that breeds contempt, but familiarity and the deliberate focus on familiar faults. This familiarity combined with bad habit can be so harmful to the family.[19]

As to love of one's own and love of honor, these two can be exploited by the couple's decision to go both *all-in* and *all-out*. By going "all-in," I mean the spouses should give themselves entirely to one another. They should regularly give their very bodies to one another, and thus foster the sense of a mutual extension of the body—the two becoming one flesh. For like reason, the man should declare himself, fully and completely, without reservation, the man of the woman. The woman, in turn, should declare herself fully the man's woman. And they should

---

their offspring; conventional marriage puts the father's very name on the offspring and establishes a strong "presumption of paternity" that any child born to his wife is indeed his offspring. Adoptive parents acquire a similar passionate attachment by a similar conventional designation. And in both cases, natural and adoptive parents deepen their attachments by the personal investment they put into the children. But here too biological mothers take the lead, because from the beginning they put so much of themselves in the babies they carry.

19 And of course, one should avoid focusing one's attention on the qualities of other attractive men and women. That's why the old-fashioned wedding vows included this promise: to willfully *forsake* all others.

otherwise invest lavishly in the marriage. Indeed, they should jump into marriage with all four feet. Stated otherwise, they should get on that "bicycle built for two," committing all four feet to the enterprise and "'ped'ling away down the road of life."[20]

By going all-out they should make this promise in front of many, many people. They should invite many friends whose opinions they value. Even more, they should invite the whole society to the wedding, that is, get the "piece of paper," to further bind the promise up.

And after so doing, the spouses should make and preserve close friendships with people who will encourage and even applaud their efforts. Married people usually need friends who are friends to marriage, and especially friends to *their* marriage.

—————·—————

But we're getting ahead of ourselves just a bit. Before getting hitched, we must begin the work of mutual attraction.

---

20  Harry Dacre, *Daisy Bell (Bicycle Built for Two)* (1892).

# CHAPTER SIX

## *HOW TO PROCEED: DANCING WITH NATURE*
### (*OR* WIFE-AND-HUSBAND HUNTING 101)

Let me begin this chapter with two important disclaimers. First, there is no promise that if you follow these steps you will successfully attract a husband or wife. There are no guarantees in life except death. Further, as Jane Austen noted, in "matrimonial affairs" there is a "luck" that "so often defies anticipation."[1] Planning and enterprise are usually a necessary condition for marriage. But luck sometimes is decisive: some great marriages arise almost haphazardly, while the best planning and efforts will not always result in any marriage.

Second, and more importantly, let me warn the reader that these steps should not be followed if you do not want to get married. Marriage is often rather easy to fall into, for as Aristotle wrote, men and women are by nature inclined to live in pairs. Therefore, once you do this dance with Nature, you run the grave risk that some man or woman will want to go home with you—permanently—and that you will be inclined to the same.

In other words, *don't try this at home unless you want a marital home.*

But if you are incurably marriage-minded, convinced that such a home is something you'd like to come home to, read this chapter. If you follow these steps for a year or two, your marital prospects will likely improve significantly.

---

1    Jane Austen, *Emma* (Mineola, NY: Dover Pubs., 2012), 108.

## A. Fix your attitude—in five steps

### 1. Resolve to put appetite in its place.

In aspiring to marriage, you are planning an enduring relationship with another human being, maybe even for a whole lifetime. This enterprise will likely be the most important decision in your life.

What role should *appetite* play? Appetite will typically have an important place, for mutual attraction is an important component of marriage. Marriage usually begins with mutual attraction, and marriage thrives on such attraction. Therefore you must resolve to give mutual attraction its due and rightful place. But where is that place?

The answer requires appreciating that marriage is a unity, where the marital unity depends on the spouses' personal unity. A strong marriage is composed of strong people. Marital integrity depends, in turn, on the spouses' personal integrity—*wholeness*. Stated otherwise, a whole marriage requires a whole woman and a whole man.

Personal integrity, in its turn, requires that each person's major parts have their due place. This *integrity* requires prioritization. You must put first things first, last things last, and all in their proper place.

The three parts of the individual that seem critical to both personal unity and therefore marital unity are as follows: (1) the mind, (2) the heart, and (3) the body.

The mind. The most important part is our mind. We are homo *sapiens*—knowing animals. The mind is, or should be, the governing part. There we develop and hold our fundamental beliefs, and seek out the true, the good, and the beautiful. Pursue marriage only with individuals who share your most deeply-held convictions; those might be religious, political, philosophical, or otherwise.

In identifying your deepest convictions, think about your deepest aspirations. *What kind of man or woman do you aspire to be?* Think—and think hard—on this question. Then ask, if children might be in your plans: *What kind of man or woman do I hope my son or daughter will be?*

Think—and think hard—on this question.

These are the most important questions in deciding both whether and whom to marry. Only get married if you think marriage will help get you there. Therefore, only marry someone who is going in the same direction as you. Although you will never find perfect agreement with anyone else, you can and should seek mutual agreement on some core, non-negotiable beliefs.

And for heaven's sake, if you want an enduring, lifelong marriage, choose someone who shares your resolution to stick together, come hell or high water. Marriage is sometimes difficult: pick someone who's resolved to work and fight for it.

This unity of the mind—common aspirations and convictions—is by far the most important to personal and marital happiness. *Do not compromise here.*

The heart. The second most important part is the heart. Affection, emotion, etc.—these are all essential elements of human nature. Pursue marriage only with someone whose company you enjoy. You'll be spending a lot of time together—make sure you like being with him or her. It should be pleasant. It won't be regularly euphoric, but it can and should be generally pleasant, sometimes very pleasant.

The body. The third most important part is the body, including its sexual appetite—the main subject of this book. It is the least important of the three, but it is by no means unimportant. Pursue marriage with someone only if you think that sleeping with that person will be pleasant. Here too, don't expect to find anyone who will guarantee "mind-blowing" pleasure on a regular basis. That's not possible and it's not good for marriage. You'd forget to eat, work, pay the rent, etc. Still, the marriage bed is a place of a pleasant, sometimes very pleasant, embrace. That's your goal.

In this regard, do not expect or demand that you, or your future spouse, perform some self-lobotomy. Do not demand, of yourself or your partner, an indifference or hostility to attraction. Our bodies are an essential part of the package deal that makes us who we are. Therefore, our bodies are an essential part of the package deal that is marriage.

Be honest about your own natural desires. Be honest about what the opposite sex wants. Be honest with the facts of mutual bodily attraction. Hopefully, after reading this far, you are now far better equipped to do this.

### 2. Resolve to please the opposite sex by bending, but not breaking.

Your next resolution—strangely controversial in our times—is to be pleasing. Do what you can, within reason, to make yourself pleasing to the opposite sex. Reach out a little bit across the great sex divide. Resolve to meet the man or the woman halfway (or even just a little way). *Bend.*

It is amazing in our time how much anger this suggestion can provoke. It's a sign of the mutual alienation and hostility of the sexes. Women should please men?!? But men should try to please women, and yes, women should try to please men. The marital enterprise requires such bending. Husbands and wives need to try a little to please one another. And aspiring spouses need to do the same.

Some of the revulsion at the thought of pleasing someone else seems to arise from the cult of *authenticity*. I don't want to *change* for anyone. I want to be myself.

In some respects, this stubbornness is good. Human nature, our personal temperaments, and habits are what they are, and no one should try to break himself or herself in order to be attractive. Indeed, such self-destruction actually makes individuals less attractive and even unfit for marriage. And above all, never sacrifice your deepest convictions on the marital altar.

But a stubborn refusal to bend is equally inhuman and anti-marital. Marriage is a community and requires that its members bend a little.

Who are you, really? Recall that you are, truly, a product of millions of years of male-female bonds, the vast majority of which involved freedom, some pleasure, and a common home. Your ancestors, male and female, figured this out over and over again. This made you. This is who you are.

But if deep down, you are a being utterly unwilling to bend, compromise, change in any way (not matter how small or peripheral), then you are unfit for marriage. Of course, most people really aren't like that. They just fail to distinguish between *bending* and *breaking*. They fear any *bending* will mean *breaking*. They are desperately afraid that personal compromise of any sort will mean personal disintegration.

But the distinction, for the most part, is easy to see. Sit down and take stock of yourself: What are your essentials—those truly non-negotiable aspects of yourself—and where are your peripheral habits, likes, dislikes, etc.? Be honest here. Changing the first would be a *breaking*. Changing the second would be a *bending*.

Let me cite one example of how this works. When I was a bachelor, I never bought flowers. I never cared for a minute about the presence or absence of flowers in my apartment. That's "who I was"—I was a non-floral man. Conversely, however, I liked bacon a lot.

Now at length I got hitched to someone unlike me. She was floral by nature; she liked flowers, and she liked receiving them from me. Conversely, she had far less enthusiasm for bacon. She was a floral non-bacon person.

After we got married, we compromised, we bent, we (gulp) *changed*. I thought, you know, even though I'm not very floral, my wife is, and I should *change* for her. My wife *changed*; she brings home bacon, and gets out of the way while I fry it up in a pan. We get along. We bend a bit. And after a while the bending can become a habit. It starts to feel free and easy and even pleasant. It's not scary, I promise.

Now let's consider how I did not *break*. I am naturally very loquacious—I like to talk a lot (too much, in fact). If my wife was incurably attracted to the "strong, silent" type, then she would have made a grave mistake in marrying me; and I would have made a grave mistake in trying to fit into such a mould.

So be resolved to bend but not break. Such bending is necessary to the marital enterprise from the beginning till the end. But don't try to break yourself.

Another way to distinguish bending from breaking is with this rule: Are you becoming a better man or woman—a better version of yourself— or are you disintegrating? When I buy my wife flowers, I'm becoming a better man, and not disintegrating. I'm doing something *different* but *beneficial* to me, my wife, and our home.

Stated otherwise, to enter Club Marriage, the sign says "No Straitjacket Required—or Permitted." You must be free. You must bend. And you must not break.

### 3. Resolve not to settle for fantasy when you can have reality.

*Won't have to make up any more stories*
*You'll be there!*
*Think of the bright midsummer night glories*
*We can share.*
*Won't have to go on kissing a daydream*
*I'll have you*
*You'll be real*
*Real as the white moon lighting the blue.*[2]

Men and women like to fantasize. And when they fantasize they make up fantasies. Those fantasies can be phantoms that could never exist. They're cartoons: mere images of men and women who are absurdly attractive, absurdly undemanding, and conversely, absurdly flexible— they bend entirely to serve our whims and ease. At the same time, these gods and goddesses are inexplicably ravenous with desire for our stubborn, lazy mediocrity.

After wallowing in these fantasies, men and women look over at real men and women and sigh. They're so unattractive. They have

---

2    Oscar Hammerstein II, *Oklahoma!* (1943). Or as somebody wrote, "Whoso findeth a wife findeth a good thing" (Proverbs 18:22).

blemishes. Even worse, they make demands, and they're not very flexible. Unlike the fantasies, these real people have *bones* as well as *flesh*, so their flexibility is quite limited.

Sometimes the dreamers then resolve not to "settle" for such earthlings. Their resolutions get even more firm by the urgings of their lazy friends of the same sex. Single-sex groups assemble, debate, and unanimously concur in the resolution: the other sex is a great disappointment.

The fantasizers have it entirely backwards. Real men and women are vastly superior to cartoons. First and foremost, real men and women have the distinctive advantage of being real, not fake.[3] *We* make dreams, dreams don't make us. We are the real *stuff* that dreams are made on, as Shakespeare once wrote.[4]

Instead of wallowing in fantasies, the aspiring husband and wife must resolve, with fierce determination, not to settle for some mere fantasy when reality is possible. Set aside your vulgar and fraudulent fantasies, whether found in porn, romance novels, or elsewhere. Put away your dumb cartoons—they're not even fit for children.

Stop being so lazy. Go wife fishing. Go husband hunting. Aim really high.

### 4. Resolve to proceed as a happy warrior—with joy and confidence.

*Refusons tous deux que nos lendemains soient mornes et gris.*
*Nous attendrons l'heure de notre bonheur.*
*Toi ma destinée, je saurais t'aimer.*
*J'en ai rêvé.*[5]

---

3    On the superiority of the real over the fake, consider this comment by a philosopher: The "personal awakening to the wonder of being," that is "an existential awakening to what it means to be" can arise from a variety of experiences, including the "intense love experience: the wonder and delight that so-and-so is truly real." W. Norris Clarke, S.J., *The One and the Many: A Contemporary Thomistic Metaphysics* (Notre Dame, IN: University of Notre Dame Press, 2000), 27–28.

4    William Shakespeare, *The Tempest*: 4.1.157.

5    "Let the two of us refuse to accept that our tomorrows will be sad and gray. / We'll await the hour of our happiness. / You, my destiny, I'll know how to love you. / I

As we set forth in the prior chapter, you have abundant reason for confidence. It is highly likely that you are already well equipped to succeed in the enterprise of mutual attraction. It is highly likely that you can both please and be pleased. You've been bred to do this thing for millions of years.

You should, therefore, proceed as a happy warrior—with joy and confidence. Both are infectious, and both are very attractive.

Armed with such joy and confidence, you will be much more likely to see the beauty of the world, both in yourself and in the people you encounter.

Human beings are funny. Both men and women get stuck in a rut. We say, with Groucho Marx: "I don't want to belong to any club that will accept me as a member." We've got it backwards. It's more true and more effective to recall as follows: "I AM God's gift to a man or a woman, and he or she will be a gift to me." Go out there. Resolve to be that gift. Resolve to receive that gift.

### 5. Resolve to be patient and kind.

All this joy and confidence might make you impatient. And it might make you reckless toward others' feelings.

Be patient. It takes time. When Mama said, "you can't hurry love," she was basically right. You can hurry it some but not much. My rough estimate: on average and in general, if you follow the steps of this chapter, you will see some improvement within a year, and will substantially improve your chances that marriage will occur within three to five years.

And be kind. Everyone, both male and female, has vulnerabilities. Too often we become absorbed with our own insecurities and sensitivities. Try to remember others' feelings as you proceed. Resolve that you will take care not to needlessly embitter someone else's future wife or

---

dreamed about it." Natacha Nahon, *J'en ai Rêvé* (1959). Adaptation of Sammy Fain & Jack Lawrence, *Once Upon a Dream* (1959).

husband. We have more than enough bitterness out there. We could use a lot more kindness.

At the end of this chapter—in the last step for both sexes—I will elaborate on the importance of kindness in marital pursuits.

## B. Looking around—in three steps

Having adjusted your attitude, now you can start looking around.

### 1. Go where the getting is good.

First you have to go where the getting is good. The getting is horrible in your living room or bedroom. You need to venture outside. There are plenty of fish in the sea, but they won't fly through your window.

In prioritizing your spouse-hunting activities, put first things first. Remember the first union—the union of the mind. Go to those places where are you likely to meet single men and women who share your common core values, beliefs, etc.

If some nonprofit is your passion, spend time there. If religion is your primary belief, go where those who share your religious priorities are. If politics is most important to you, get involved. If a commercial activity is your joy, then get involved in a trade organization. Be a joiner. But make sure there are some single people around.

Next, remember the second union—the union of the heart. Think about where you are likely to meet single men and women who share your diversions, hobbies, etc. Here too—get involved in fun activities.

Overall, if you can, get involved in at least two or three distinct significant activities where you are likely to find single people who share your fundamental beliefs and pastimes.

Oftentimes people do the opposite. They go where they think they'll find the most attractive people, and then hope that one of those attractive types will also shares their beliefs or hobbies. More foolishly, some hope to find a husband or wife at a place devoted to the casual hook-up. It can happen, but it's rare.

Instead, prioritize what you should prioritize. Consider first your deepest convictions and aspirations. Then think about your interests and hobbies. Worry about your bodily appetites last.

And do make full use of the benefits of online services—where you can look for single people who share your passions, interests, beliefs, and the rest. But try to limit your searches to someone within a reasonable travel distance from you; you'll need to be able to spend quality time with any potential spouse. Further, make sure to mention the word "marriage" prominently in your profile. Don't be shy here: you'll attract the marriage-minded and turn away the very un-marriage-minded. Anyone who's allergic to the word "marriage" is simply not marriage-minded and not worth your dating time.

Cast a very wide net. There really are plenty of fish in the sea.

### 2. Open your eyes and look.

So now that you've gotten to the right places, open your eyes and look.

In this business of mutual attraction, there is a twofold work. One must make an effort to be *attractive*, to be sure. But one must also make some effort to be *attracted*. Vis-à-vis eligible singles, you must focus not only on looking good, but also on looking at their attractive features.

This second effort is frequently overlooked. According to the legend and lore, love comes "at first sight." Overpowering beauty is what we expect. But that's not how it works usually. Typically you must make some efforts: you must choose to see before you can enjoy.

So first, find some single men or women who may fit the basic criteria of the first union—of the mind. Second, among these, see if any are enjoyable company, allowing for the second union—of the heart.

Third, among these people, look for attractive features. Gentlemen, be on the lookout for the woman whose smile is infrequent because she is shy, or merely superficially edgy. Look for women who may have a crust, but a thin crust. There are many such women.

Ladies, try to notice strengths that a man has not displayed. Lots of men don't display well, sometimes from lack of know-how or some easily-curable insecurity.

It is in this area where both men and women *can* easily change, some with a little bit of effort on their part, or a bit of encouragement from others. That second or third look at thinly veiled beauty can trigger a strong attraction.

Of course, here and elsewhere, bend but don't break. Many people will simply not be attractive to you despite your efforts. Just make some effort here and see how it goes.

In general, the more you make a point of noticing others' attractive qualities, you will begin to see an increase in the number of attractive people.[6] The harvest is rich—really rich.

And please resist the unhelpful whining: Why should I have to look more? It's *their* job to open up a little, smile more readily, lose a few pounds, show some manliness etc., etc., etc.

No. Stop wasting your time casting blame across the sex divide; reach out just a little bit—not even half way, even just a quarter of the way. If both sexes did so, Nature can easily build the rest of the bridge.

### 3. Guard your heart.

The more you open your eyes, the more you'll understand the old adage, "guard your heart." The problem with attraction is not that love

---

6    I can think of more than one young woman who fit this description: She had a somewhat melancholic disposition; she was smart, kind, but not immediately attractive, mainly because her shyness or thin crust kept her from displaying that ready smile and easy laughter that is so lovely in women. But an intrepid young man had his eyes open—and pursued. The young lady grew confident, opened up, and beamed. Decades later, she remained very beautiful—the kind of woman that some men think only exist in dreams. Gentlemen, such women are real. Look around. I can think of more than one young man whose stumbling nervousness betrayed a hidden strength and kindness that make for a lovely husband. Ladies—open your eyes.

is blind; rather, love is too intensely sighted. We often can't process such intense beauty; among other difficulties, we get tunnel vision and can't see problems. Once you've had the vision of another's beauty, detachment can be brutal, precisely because you've seen something dazzling that is very, very good (even if only incomplete). Anyone who's loved deeply and lost knows this vision and this pain.

You must resist the urge to throw your heart in too soon, for two main reasons. First, the person, no matter how dazzling in one respect, may not be good for you in other respects. Second, you must give the other person the opportunity to get to know you well enough before he or she should prudently decide to reciprocate the interest. Before giving in to affection, wait until you have good reason to believe (1) that the man or woman in question is someone you should want to marry AND (2) that he or she might prudently reciprocate your well-considered marital interest.

Don't yield to love too soon. You'll need time and patience: enough time for you to prudently consider whether to surrender to love; and enough time for your partner to make the same decision.

This prudence, this reserve, is not playing hard to get. This reserve is just good judgment.

It turns out, both men and women find displays of this prudential reserve very attractive. Consider this advice that "Miss Manners" once gave as to how to look during the initial stages of courtship:

> The first thing you must learn to control is that impulse to tell [him or her] exactly how you feel....For reasons she does not pretend to understand, the obvious adoration of someone to whom you have not already been forming your own feeling of love produces distaste, rather than reciprocation, in the love object. Cheerful friendliness, along with the vaguest of looks that suggest one's feelings could grow, is the standard at which to aim.[7]

That's very good advice for your insides as well. Open your eyes just

---

7   Judith Martin (Miss Manners), "Creation of Uncertainty is What is Needed Here," *St. Petersburg Times*, Apr. 2, 1980.

enough to be cheerful, friendly, curious, ready to be pleased, but guard your heart until the right time.

And in answer to Miss Manners's query, I think the reason for our distaste for the premature adulator is that love of prudence infuses our very desires. We think, "That silly person doesn't know me well enough to adore me!" And our appetites say, more profoundly, "How is such a senseless person going to help raise our offspring?" We naturally dislike the premature (and thus imprudent) worshiper because sexual desire looks toward adult offspring; the care and education of such persons requires a good deal of prudence.

But love is impatient with prudence. We are eager for the plunge. But the only smart way to go about it is to jump in together—four feet at once. And you have to wait for that. That's what marriage is for.

*On eye-opening and heart-guarding in marriage.*

Incidentally, these habits of eye-opening and heart-guarding will serve you well in marriage. Once hitched, your job will be to make a habit of noticing the qualities of your spouse.[8] Conversely, in fulfilling your duty to "forsake all others," you will need to be on guard against the occasional initial affections that you might have for others. You must open your eyes toward your spouse's qualities, and guard your heart against others' charms.

The difference will be this: in pursuing marriage, your job will be to open your eyes to the many and guard your heart against the one; in marriage, however, your job will be to open your eyes to the one, and guard your heart against the many.[9] Moreover, in marriage, the work of opening your eyes to your spouse will be much harder than guarding your heart against outsiders; only small and occasional efforts will be

---

8    As someone wrote in the Middle Ages, "*Ubi amor, ibi oculus.*" (Where love is, there is the eye). Looking and loving go together.

9    I once heard of a wedding toast in which the best man half-jokingly said, "Just remember, what was a sin last night is a duty tonight." In some respects, that's how it works with the pre-marital and post-marital duties of eye-opening and heart-guarding.

needed to put aside the random initial affections that you may have for other men or women.[10] The harder part, often overlooked, is the work in noticing the goodness of your partner. In good marriages, spouses make these efforts regularly.

## C. Attracting a wife—in eight steps

In following these steps, remember to bend and not break. These are not "rules." Skip the steps you find impossible, improvise where necessary. Do your best.

### 1. Show confidence.

Women like strength. So be strong, or at least appear to be strong.

Easier said than done, you will rightly say. But begin with the easiest form of strength to display and even fake: strength of personality, or confidence. If you don't have one already, develop a mild, modest swagger in your walk and your talk.

And don't believe some women's denials—the vast majority of women really like this stuff. And ignore the ridicule of some downright mean women. They have issues. They're not your friends, or the friends of your future wife. It's her affection and esteem that should interest you.

It really doesn't matter if you're feeling insecure. Just fake it. Women fake stuff all the time. They put on makeup, wear padded bras, and do all sorts of things to give illusions of youth and fertility. You should do the same, by putting on fake confidence and other illusions of strength. And as you probably already know, the more you feign confidence, the more you acquire real confidence.

*Make believe you're brave*
*And the trick will take you far.*
*You may be as brave*
*As you make believe you are.*[11]

---

10  Don't believe for a moment the adulterers' protest that they just "fell in love." Such people refused to set aside the incipient affections and chose instead to cultivate them. They decided to dig the ditch, slide down, and wallow in their disgrace.

11  Oscar Hammerstein II, *The King and I* (1951).

So proceed, "fighting with growing confidence," as Churchill once said.

Like women, however, you should be moderate in your display. Too much makeup makes a woman look unattractive. Too much confidence makes a man look ridiculous. It's hard to dictate how much is too much. Just keep trying, and you'll find your balance. If you can, find a mentor; seek out trustworthy advice.

To adorn your confidence, put on a strong smile and a strong, friendly voice. Give everyone you meet, male and female, young and old, a strong, kind "hello." And try hard to remember people's names. The combination is very appealing to women: it's a combination of strength and kindness—pretty much any sensible woman's definition of an attractive man. Never forget, however, that strength is the foundation, and the smile is the decoration. A smile without strength will not attract women.

Practice makes perfect. Keep trying. Do what you can.

### 2. Display strength in other ways.

Besides friendly confidence, there are other strengths that may be at your disposal. First, identify your own strengths. As we mentioned, the average man is not average in everything. You probably have some other strength: intelligence, conversation, sociability, wealth, height, musculature, etc.

After identifying your strengths, figure out how to display them in those places where the getting is good. If you're good, say, at repairing computers, find some way to volunteer your services at the nonprofit staffed by attractive single women. Countless other examples could be given. You'll need to do some thinking and planning here.

Next, identify those other areas where you can readily increase your strength. Probably the most important strength to develop is economic strength. Women understandably look to a man's economic standing for two closely related reasons: both the subrational appetite for strength, discussed in a previous chapter, and the rational conclusion that resources will be necessary to help her in raising the offspring she might desire. For your part, it will be therefore very helpful and prudent for you to get a job, keep a job, and otherwise find a way to advance economically. You will thereby make yourself more attractive and more prepared to shoulder the burdens if you and your wife have offspring. Do your best to act and look like a good provider: marriage-minded women will like this. Believe me: if a man goes from poor to gainfully employed, he will go from nearly invisible to very visible in the eyes of many women.

Far less important, but not unimportant, is increased physical strength. The main benefits of exercise are of course not changes in your appearance. You should exercise to improve your health primarily. Exercise will help, though, by augmenting the manly friendliness in your stride and voice through more testosterone, endorphins, and a sense of accomplishment (which builds confidence).

Adding some muscle and decreasing body fat can't hurt, either. Remember that the shape of your "figure" is simply not as important to the woman as hers is to you. A six-figure salary (if you can get there!) is *far* more alluring than six-pack abs; in fact, even a $600/week salary will take your further.

Prioritize your efforts here. Focus on faking confidence, making some money, and displaying your particular strengths before women of interest.

Finally, be a gentleman. Offer little acts of physical service to all women, especially the elderly. Hold doors, offer to carry boxes, etc. There is no need here for grand ceremony or perfect etiquette. These little acts allow you to display both strength and kindness—the magic combination. And as for the angry reactions from *some* women, be a gentlemen again, and defer (don't argue with angry women—you'll always lose). But don't let their reactions confuse you: the loud angry ones are (thankfully) not representative of all women, and especially not marriage-minded women. Your principal job is to please the marriage-minded rather than appease the perpetually indignant.

*Importance of relative strength*

In this matter of strength, don't forget that women often assess it by relation or comparison. Women's appetites are frequently governed by *comparison*. It is not that a man must be strong according to some absolute standard; rather he should be strong in relation to the other men in sight.

In *Emma*, Jane Austen shows how drawing such comparisons before a woman's eye can foster or undermine a man's attractiveness. On the one hand, when Emma seeks to turn her friend's interest away from one man, she skillfully emphasizes that man's inferiority relative to other men:

> "[Mr. Martin] is very plain, undoubtedly — remarkably plain: — but that is nothing, compared with his entire want of gentility. I had no right to expect much, and I did not expect much; but I had no idea that he could be so very clownish, so totally without air. I had imagined him, I confess, a degree or two nearer gentility."

> "To be sure," said Harriet, in a mortified voice, "he is not so genteel as real gentlemen."

> "I think, Harriet, since your acquaintance with us, you have been repeatedly in the company of some, such very real gentlemen, that you must yourself be struck with the difference in Mr. Martin. At Hartfield you have had very good specimens of well educated, well bred men. I should be surprized if, after seeing them, you could be in company with Mr. Martin again without perceiving him to be a very inferior creature—and rather wondering at yourself for having ever thought him at all agreeable before."[12]

Well played, Emma. Nothing will turn the woman's switch to the "off" position faster than the "inferior creature."

Conversely, Emma's own eye is drawn toward Mr. Knightley (her eventual love interest), especially when he looks so good by comparison. At the dance, Mr. Knightley decided to hang out with some old men: "He could not have appeared to greater advantage perhaps any where,

---

12   Jane Austen, *Emma* (Mineola, NY: Dover Pubs., 2012), 20.

than where he had placed himself. His tall, firm, upright figure, among the bulky forms and stooping shoulders of the elderly men, was such as Emma felt must draw every body's eyes."[13]

What then should you do? Seek to create circumstances where you can, in Miss Austen's words, "appear to greater advantage"—that is, where you look good in comparison with the men around you. Don't constantly engage in activities where you look like a loser. Instead, compete where you can excel at least some of the time.

In this regard, the assistance of allies (wingmen) can be most helpful. At their best, these guys agree to make you look good. They agree to compliment you within the hearing of women and otherwise make you *appear* to be a winner. (Hopefully your wingmen won't be blockheads and make it all too obvious.) But even if your allies aren't very artful, the average young woman of sense will probably be impressed that you have the friends willing to make the effort. Having friends is an important strength that can trigger attraction.

### 3. Look half-way decent.

Your appearance is not unimportant. Bathe. Try not to smell. Try to dress neatly. Shave or groom your beard. Trim the nose hair. Show a modest degree of concern with your attire. Women get annoyed when they make extraordinary efforts and men seem to make none at all.

But don't overdo it. Women want to look prettier than their partners, and they find it off-putting if you outdo them, either in effort or effect. Don't give the impression that you give more attention to skin care or similar matters than she does. At a semi-conscious level, she'll consider it unmanly, mildly insulting, or both.

As for your weight, remember that women by nature are looking for help. Here's a rule of thumb: if your healthcare provider says that your weight is seriously impairing your health, then it's probably seriously impairing your allure. Remember that her appetite is looking for a helpmate in the laborious enterprise of offspring (regardless of whether

---

13  *Ibid.*, 218.

she actually wants them). Do what you can here, both to preserve your health and attract a wife. But bend, don't break.

### 4. Proceed with gentle persistence.

Now that you're getting the hang of appearing strong, you can consider taking that bold step—making some initial romantic gestures. There are different ways to proceed here—developing friendships and dating are the most common. But regardless of how you proceed, do so with gentle persistence.

By *gentle persistence* I mean cultivating a joyful, easy, but regular interest in young women. Guard your heart against the one—don't plunge into any premature infatuation—and be open to the many. Give yourself the chance to get to know young women, and for them to get to know you. Along the way, maintain that posture recommended by Miss Manners: both inside and out maintain a cheerful friendliness but with the vaguest of looks that suggest your interest could grow.

At some point, your persistence must be a little less gentle, because you will probably need to make some definitive romantic offer, like a request for a date, however casual. At some point later, you'll probably need to offer something exclusive—up to and including an engagement. Gentle persistence will aid you in both stages. As for asking for dates, a joyful but gentle posture will make young women feel more comfortable saying "yes." It will also make it easier for you to handle rejection: remember—she doesn't know you well enough to truly reject you in any meaningful way.

And finally—but of great importance—this gentle persistence will prepare you for a bit of persistence toward a particular someone. If, after significant reflection, you are convinced that a woman's first rejection was just too hasty, that mutual attraction might be good and possible, then try this approach. First, perform a tactical retreat: give her and you some space and time to think and breathe—maybe two months or more. Give your appetite and heart a rest at the same time. But maintain that cheerful friendliness and continue to otherwise display strength. If you're still incurably interested, then ask again, with that easy smile that you've been learning to fake. After the second rejection, retreat again and *maybe* repeat…for a third and last time. After the third rejection of you cheerful requests, move on: she can't see what you see. Further persistence is a waste of her time and energy and yours.

Such gentle persistence in the face of initial rejection has led to many good marriages. Sometimes the gentle persistence is required in the early stages of dating, sometimes at the proposal. Believe me, I have some reason to know.

But gentle persistence, in the main, will not involve focused persistence toward the one, but persistence among the many. Multiply your friendships. Ask many girls out for casual dates of coffee or lunch. Be prepared for lots of rejections—and try to laugh off the sting.

All this general but easy affection is so much easier if you open your eyes and guard your heart. And as you probably can guess, this freedom is easier if you are not promiscuous with sex.

### 5. Control yourself sexually.

There are several reasons why you should generally refrain from promiscuous sex, porn, and masturbation, to the extent you can.

As to promiscuous sex, it will be in tension with your marital enterprise. Habits of promiscuity are simply incompatible with actual marriage. If you are one of the few men with the skills, attributes, and habits of a Casanova,[14] marriage probably isn't for you. You'll need to break these habits, and break them for good if you're going to get married. Adultery is very bad.

It's unlikely, however, that you are such a man. Few men succeed here, and few of these are marriage-minded. You are more likely to have habits of porn and/or masturbation. It's important that you try to recede from, if not break, such habits, and for three reasons. First, they make you less attractive to women because *you* know the habits

---

14 The aptly named "Casanova" was always going from one new "*casa*" to another. If your aspiration is marriage, then your goal is to bind yourself freely to one *casa*—to be house-bound, a *hus-band.*

are contemptible, and self-contempt will make you feel less manly and thus you will appear less manly. Even worse, if she knows you have such habits, she will see you as less manly and thus less attractive. No woman fantasizes about a man downloading porn and masturbating. The actress staring back at you on the screen has nothing but contempt for you. She has less respect for you than she does for herself (if that's even possible).

Second, the habits make you less attractive because regular masturbation decreases your available libido and testosterone. Women by nature are attracted to a man who shows some spring in his step, as it were. The hormones, the pheromones, all help to give you that step.

Third, regular porn and masturbation make you less attracted to real women. You lose not only the libido but even the inclination to real women. Regular exposure to cartoonish images and scenarios can make you insensitive to real flesh-and-blood women. Consuming porn is like eating artificial jalapeños with artificial concentrations of spice. Just as such fake food can make the taste buds grow numb to real food, porn and masturbation can make you go blind to real women—just like the old wives suggested. Real ice cream and bacon are better than fake jalapeños, and real women are better than cartoons.[15]

The good news, however, is that abstinence can have a significant effect in restoring manliness. Try to figure out a way to break away from these habits. There is substantial information available online to help you break or diminish these habits.[16] You'll like yourself more. You'll like real women more. And real women will like you more.

### 6. Let her be and appear chaste.

Be honest here. Recall that your desire for a wife is shaped in part by her appearance of reliability. A woman's apparent reserve, if not chastity, is closely related to her appeal to you. At the same time, the woman will

---

15  And when the time comes, all this self-numbing undermines performance. Erectile dysfunction is apparently widespread among young men today.

16  Some of the websites include "Fight the New Drug," "NoFap," and "Purity is possible." I'm sure there are many others.

deeply wish, at some level, to appear chaste in her husband's eyes; *no* woman wants her beloved to consider her a slut. Remember that men and women have evolved together: in large measure, what you want to do she wants you to do, and vice-versa.

To preserve and cultivate mutual attraction, you will have to play your part in safeguarding her appearance of chastity. The task will be twofold. First, as you proceed toward marriage, put a veil over her sexual past—whether sex, pornography, masturbation, or otherwise. Don't be overly curious for details. Ask for, and accept, her reassurance that she has been and will be devoted to marital fidelity. She will assure you more by her actions than her words.

Second, don't put pressure on her to do something that will ultimately make her less attractive. Your potential wife may well yield to you long before you've made any kind of commitment. As you project strength, as I've recommended, she will yield to you more readily. Apart from bodily desire, the woman may yield simply from the natural human desire to please or from the natural fear of rejection. Remember: women are not made of steel.

Instead, mutually agree on a rule, a line that should not be crossed. If you both make and observe such a rule, you will signal to each other, at a rational and subrational level, your mutual seriousness. Your mutual respect for this limit will thus nurse your mutual affection. I discuss some possible "limits" below.

In this regard, there is something of an analogue in women's relationship to men: where men need to hold the line and women need to back off. A woman sometimes can make demands on a boyfriend where compliance would make the man less attractive in her eyes. To be sure, as a general rule, it's good to be pleasing and helpful. But at some point some demands will become unreasonable: don't yield to these. It's a great mistake to believe that obedience to every one of her whims will make you appear more attractive. Don't believe it. Servility is very unattractive.

Where should you draw the line? A few examples could include: asking you to do maintenance or cleaning jobs at her house, watching her kids, or borrowing money. These services belong in marriage for the most part. She is wrong to make the demand, and you would be foolish to comply. Despite her protests to the contrary, you will look less attractive to her if you give in. Remember: women like strength, and they become disinterested in a man who will share his best resources—his time and talents—whenever some woman bats her eyelashes at him. Instead, tell her this with firmness and kindness: "If you become my wife, I will do this and all manner of other services for you for the rest of my life. We need first to put on a ring on it." You will appear much more attractive. You'll like each other more that way.

Now reconsider your immediate sexual appetites. Be *honest* here—will she truly be more or less attractive tomorrow if you persuade her to yield tonight? Your subrational appetite, recall, is looking for a woman who will *not* give in to the charms of the next hot guy that comes alone (and surely you know that you're not that awesome, right?). If she tells you to put a ring on it, happily agree. You'll like each other more that way.

### 7. Appeal to auxiliary appetites—food, flowers, and dancing

Sex is an appetite. But it's not the only appetite. And the appetites are not segregated from one another They have a strange and complex interrelationship. Sometimes the appeal to one appetite affects the others. It's all very complicated, and I don't pretend to any clear understanding here.

Still, let's begin with the primary and most powerful appetite: for food. Women and men like to eat, even more than they like to have sex. (Try abstaining from both). In some subtle ways, food stimulates the sexual desire. Providing food to a woman can make you appear more attractive as a man.

At first, of course, you should not provide a focused gift—that's going too far. Instead, feed groups of people that happen to include single women. Host dinner parties. Be the guy who brings donuts to the meeting. Think about the ways to please women without prematurely showing excessive interest in the one.

Parenthetically, note that food serves a different function if you're exceptionally good at cooking. Here the provision of food will serve primarily as a display of strength—a more direct way to a woman's heart.

As you proceed toward marriage, it will be helpful to focus your food deliveries. Provide her with food. Buy her chocolates (you do know that women like chocolate, right?). This custom of chocolates developed for a reason: proven efficacy.

A second appetite that women have is the delight in looking and feeling pretty. Once you've made some progress with a particular woman, buy her flowers every once in a while. Ignore any initial eye roll. Disregard your (reasonable) fears that she's ridiculing the gift with her girlfriends. Maybe she is. For the most part, however, she won't like you less, and she'll probably like you more. Refrain only if she expressly tells you to stop bringing the flowers. Remember, *gentle persistence*.

A third appetite is the love of grace and movement. Both sexes have this inclination, but women more so. If you have the time, learn how to dance a little. Remember the goal is to help the woman feel graceful. Aim to be graceful in a way that makes her feel graceful (so, not appearing more graceful than her). This method can be quite powerful. I recall a few acquaintances of mine who were frankly unattractive in so many ways. But they displayed a bit of confidence and learned how to dance in this modest, gentlemanly way; they did quite well in the marital enterprise.

There are probably other appetites that can be your allies. But these three are probably the most potent. Use them to your advantage if you can.

### 8. Be promiscuous with your kindness.

This last step is common to both men and women. I discuss it below.

## D. Attracting a husband—in eight steps

I repeat and emphasize here precisely what I said to the men. In following these steps, remember to bend and not break. These are not "rules." Skip the steps you find impossible, and improvise where necessary. Do your best.

### 1. Smile.

*"Joy is the best makeup. Joy, and good lighting."* — Anne Lamott.[17]

By far your most potent and versatile weapon is right under your nose, literally: your smile. Men have an insatiable appetite for a woman's ready and warm smile. Dante could never get enough of Beatrice's smile, which just seemed to get bigger and brighter the more he looked. Or as Oscar Hammerstein wrote, "All the world forgotten / In one woman's smile."[18]

A smile appeals strongly to men at two levels. At a rational, conscious level, the smile suggests kindness, and no sane man wants to marry an unkind woman. At a subrational level, the smile suggests the kind of patience that babies desperately need if they are ever to reach a flourishing adulthood.

Stated otherwise, men are looking for a woman who appears to suffer fools gladly. Men would like to be suffered, and most men know they are fools; only the most foolish men deny it. Furthermore, the male appetite knows that young children are fools and desperately need a mother who will suffer them.

The smile has at least two major advantages as a weapon of choice. First, it's the easiest thing to fake; and repeated faking makes the habit feel free, easy, and pleasant.

Second, there's almost no need to worry about excess. Indeed, promiscuity here is a virtue: give your smile away. In this respect, I

---

17  Anne Lamott, *Grace (Eventually): Thoughts on Faith* (New York: Penguin Publishers, 2007), 77.

18  Oscar Hammerstein II, *The Desert Song* (1926).

cannot improve on the simple advice that Margaret Kent gave in her best-selling marriage book a generation ago:

> Your smile is one of your most attractive attributes. Smiling is special, and part of the whole process of saying hello. It's fun, it's easy to do, and after all, smiles don't wear out....
>
> The first thing you must do is say hello to every man... Greet every man you are reasonably sure is not a danger to you. Treat every man as worthy of a friendly hello....Just smiling a warm hello at every man, whether he's your paperboy or your lawyer, will give you the reputation of being a friendly person and make it easier for men to approach you and meet you...
>
> [In groups, be] friendly to everyone...and never act like a snob.... Smile and say hello to all the men—and all the women too.[19]

I once heard of a plain-looking, overweight woman who had attracted a large number of attractive suitors. When friends asked her secret, she gave this simple, direct answer: "I smile a lot. I laugh a lot. And I bake a lot." Wisdom.

*Believe me*, this kind of nice works. Give it a try. I dare you.

And after all—being cheerful and kind to others is probably something we shall be doing more of anyway.

## 2. Otherwise project exclusive fertility (look like a lady).

*"Your dresses should be tight enough to show you're a woman and loose enough to show you're a lady."* — Edith Head.[20]

Besides a smile, there are several other ways to enhance your allure. They all involve ways to project fertility, and more particularly, reliably *exclusive* fertility. Looking like "a lady"—"pretty" or "feminine"—is really another way of saying, "I can offer reliably exclusive fertility."

This advice often encounters two negative reactions. The first is

---

19  Margaret Kent, *How to Marry the Man of Your Choice* (2007).

20  I have not found the original source of the quotation, but it is widely attributed to Ms. Head.

the opinion that directing women to show some, but not too much, womanhood is placing them on a perilous balance beam between a rock and a hard place. But remember that the way is broad, with lots of room to maneuver and improvise, and that male appetite grades all such matters on a very generous curve.

Here's a general helpful rule: in your dress and conduct, follow the example of young married women or other marriage-minded single women. Conversely, avoid behaving or dressing in a manner that is significantly more provocative or vulgar than most women around you. Marriage-minded men are looking, even at a subrational level, for women who dress as if they are marriage-minded; modesty is largely a function of custom.

The second negative reaction is the assertion that male standards are too demanding, and this can lead to two extreme and opposite responses. On the one hand, some women devote their lives slavishly to their appearance. On the other, others angrily disavow all such efforts and even engage in what I call "gratuitous self-homlification"[21]: deliberately dressing and acting in an unattractive way.[22]

Neither of these extremes is helpful to your marital allure. Remember, men are looking for someone who is sane as well as pretty. Remember to bend, not break. And remember to give the body its due: its subordinate and not-unimportant place.

As to the following particulars, remember to proceed with joy and confidence. Your goal is not to *cover* ugliness, but to *enhance* your existing beauty. You are already beautiful—don't forget it.

*(1) Makeup*

---

21 "Homely," however, is a slanderous cognate of the word "home." Neither the bride, nor the mother, nor the home is ugly—quite the contrary.

22 According to an anecdote I once heard, a formerly-thin woman said to her friends, in front of her husband, "Now that I'm married I don't care anymore." She proceeded to engage in some eating that a lumberjack would consider excessive. At a conscious level, the husband was surely sad, less by her extra pounds, and more by her overt contempt.

Generally, use a modest amount of makeup. The goal here is to enhance natural human beauty rather than to appear like an alien or a clown. Aliens are scary. Clowns are scarier. Don't scare the menfolk.

*(2) Hair*

Remember that in choosing a hairstyle, there are three competing interests: (1) the woman's interest in comfort and ease, (2) the hairdresser's interest in profit, and (3) the woman's interest in being attractive to men. The last one might be the least important. The first interest alone would dictate a very low maintenance buzzcut. The second interest would dictate the high-maintenance hairstyle—which is short, but with multiple layers and highlights. The third—most attractive to men—is long hair, somewhere between shoulder length to mid-back. This last one can be uncomfortable in hot climates, and it is cumbersome insofar as it sometimes requires more maintenance. Depending on race/ethnicity, it can involve even more extensive work. And it provides very little income to the hairdresser, as it requires very little professional upkeep.

To the extent to which you can endure the hassle of longer hair, and can resist the marketing and entreaties of your hairdresser, then it's a good idea to keep your hair long, whether in a ponytail or otherwise.

*(3) Clothing*

There's much that could be said here. One general standard to keep in mind is to use clothing to highlight or create the illusion of a slim waistline, which creates the appearance of the hourglass figure.

*(4) The somewhat weighty issue*

I hesitate to say anything about the "figure" or "weight," because it's such a minefield. But I promised candor, so I can't just ignore the topic.

Here goes. It's not all-important, but it's not unimportant. It would be uncandid and frankly ridiculous to pretend as if your weight didn't affect attraction at all. Any woman who once weighed 300 pounds and lost half her weight will report that men's interest in her increased dramatically. On the other hand, men generally are quite pleased with the average woman's figure.

We should distinguish two ways in which weight is weighty. First, I will repeat what I said to the men: "Here's a rule of thumb: if your healthcare provider says that your weight is seriously impairing your health, then it's probably seriously impairing your allure. Remember that her appetite is looking for a helpmate in the laborious enterprise of offspring (regardless of whether she actually wants them). Do what you can here, both to preserve your health and attract a wife." So, if you have *compelling* health-related reasons to gain or lose weight, such efforts will, as an added benefit, also substantially improve your allure.

The second way weight matters—and it's less important—is where weight is within the broad range of healthy or healthy-ish. "Figure enhancement" here will usually confer some benefit, but it will probably be small compared with the benefits of "smile enhancement" (see above). Women who are petite and carry some weight in the face or waistline will find efforts here more beneficial. I remember an attractive classmate in college. After a summer break, she returned after losing about 20 pounds (so she bragged), and appeared even more attractive. She was petite, and some padding had concealed her jaw line and waistline; so the modest weight loss did make a big difference. I recall my male classmates' quiet but evident reaction to the change.

Exercise has its own benefits apart from any figure enhancement. Besides improving your health, it helps provide some endorphins that make you feel confident and joyful—and thus more attractive, and attracted, to men.

So make some modest efforts here, if you can. Bend, but don't break.

### 3. Act like a lady.

As discussed, men's "Quantity Zone" does not tolerate a woman who gives the impression that she is too generous with her fertility. So it's important that the marriage-minded woman not give men, at a conscious or subconscious level, the false impression that she is promiscuity-minded and not marriage-minded.

Accordingly, to the extent you can, avoid vulgarity and profanity, especially profanity regarding sex. Don't speak in a manner that men cannot help but associate with the prostitute. Don't indulge in the jocular custom of calling your female friends indelicate or offensive names.

Similarly, avoid activities that are too closely related to "unreliable" women. Don't engage in cutesy imitations of stripper culture (e.g., pole-dancing "exercise" classes). Such activities have a depressing effect on men's marital interests. Don't turn your backside into a billboard celebrating how "sexy" you are. Even prostitutes don't advertise in such a ridiculous way.

Just don't do any of this stuff. The male appetite can't process this confusing message: "I just like to pretend to be a slut, but I'm not a slut...usually. Tee hee." Once the male appetite hears a word like "prostitute," you'll be banished from his Quality Zone.

Instead, aim to act in a moderately conservative way. Act more like the married and marriage-minded women you know.

### 4. Proceed with gentle persistence.

Whatever courtship ritual or custom you follow, if any, the same rule applies to you as to men: proceed with gentle persistence. Guard your heart and open your eyes—go on dates with any many men whom you think might share your convictions and aspirations. Worry about bodily attraction last. Make the dates casual, easy, pleasant—and in public, safe places. If you feel comfortable doing so, ask many guys out on such dates.

But what if he gets the wrong idea—that you're either looking for quick sex or fast marriage with him? If you're bold enough to ask a guy out for coffee, you're bold enough to tell him firmly what you intended: "Just some pleasant conversation. Nothing more." And say it with the warm smile you've been working on—the one that will suggest that *maybe* something more might be on your mind. Remember the advice above: find men with whom you think you might possible have the three unions (mind, heart body), and then maintain on the outside and the inside, that cheerful friendliness, with that posture that you might be open to something more.

In finding, attracting, and getting to know marriage-minded men, just be patient and persistent. Don't scare the men. And don't be scared of them. Even the most magnificently manly man is, in truth, only somewhat different from you. We're all humans—both sexes are from the same earth.

### 5. Control yourself sexually.

As to promiscuity, porn, and masturbation, all my advice to the aspiring husband is more or less applicable to the aspiring wife as well. If you have habits of promiscuity, you owe it to yourself and your future spouse to find a way to break those habits. As to porn and masturbation, if you break or at least recede from such habits, you'll like yourself more—you'll feel more feminine—and then you'll like real men more, and real men will like you more.

As I mentioned to the gentlemen, it is in your interest to control yourself—even and especially, with a potential spouse. We've considered the reason: men are looking for a woman who will not readily and easily share her fertility with other men. At a subrational level, at least, a man knows that other equally charming fellows are always around. Yielding to him too easily will signal that you could yield to them too easily.

As the comedian Steve Harvey has said, "Men Respect Standards—Get Some!"[23] Indeed, men's appetites *deeply* respect standards.

What should your standards be? Here are five possible rules to follow. I present them in the order of their connection with lifelong marriage.[24]

---

23 Steve Harvey, *Act Like a Lady, Think Like a Man: What Men Really Think About Love, Relationships, Intimacy, and Commitment* (expanded edition, 2014).

24 Some religious readers may insist that only the first two are acceptable based

1. No sex until a marriage for life.

2. No sex until a marriage, subject to divorce.

3. No sex until an engagement to marry for life.

4. No sex until an engagement to marry, subject to divorce.

5. No sex until a promise of pre-marital exclusivity, subject to breakup (a quasi-divorce).

Pick the rule that you think you can live by, but err on the side of greater self-control and marital permanence. Once you're getting serious with a particular man, state the rule openly. By firmly announcing and following this rule, you will signal to his appetite that you are serious about monogamy, and that you will not bring to his home children that are not his. Hold the line here: the *marriage-minded man* will like you more.[25] The *promiscuity-minded man* will like you less, but that's good; he's not going where you're going.

## 6. Let him be and appear strong.

Strength is to men what physical beauty is to women. After millions of years, men have a deep-seated desire to feel and appear strong, before others in general, before women more specifically, and before their beloved most of all. The same is true of women and their need to feel pretty. Therefore, just as it's important for a man to let a woman feel pretty, it's important for a woman to let a man feel strong.

At the very least, the marriage-minded woman should not ridicule the efforts that men make to appear strong, just as men should not ridicule

---

on principles set forth in the Bible, Quran, Upanishads, or other holy authority. My advice here, however, is directed toward the non-religious equally with the religious; I think that the other, less stringent standards can still provide significant reassurance to the male marital appetite.

25 By holding the line here, you will have other advantages: you can forego hormonal contraceptives and begin to ovulate. Ovulation makes women significantly more attractive to men. Ovulating women emit powerful pheromones; moreover, ovulation changes women's telephone voice and manner of walking in subtle ways that men detect simply by speaking on the phone or watching the women on film.

the efforts that women make to appear pretty. There is sometimes silliness and even excess in the ways in which women and men do these things. Of course women spend too much time fussing with their clothes, makeup and hair; of course men strut around too much. Of course such things are often downright funny. And often our efforts fall flat. But at a subrational and sometimes a conscious level, the opposite sex is trying to please you—even in an incomplete and imperfect way. So lay off. Don't be a jerk. Try to do the decent thing and try to be pleased.

This rule is especially important as you proceed in a particular relationship—where we become more vulnerable. Just as the man should let his potential wife appear reliable (or chaste), the woman should let her potential husband appear strong. In both cases, the aspiring spouses need to limit their demands. Do not place demands on your future husband that will, in truth, make him appear less manly to you and to himself.

The problem arises almost naturally. Women, just like men, like their own way and like to get stuff. And it's natural to ask the boyfriend for the stuff. And he will often comply, if only because people often just like to just get along, and often because you can make him miserable with your complaints.

But at some point, his compliance will tend to diminish his allure, just as the sexually adventurous girlfriend may begin to seem less marriageable. Be attentive to this problem.

In your own mind, be honest about the nature of your requests. Are you asking something that he really should do only for a wife? Are you asking him to do things that he should reserve for marriage?

In the previous section, I suggested three kinds of activities that a man should do only for a wife: watching her children, cleaning her house, and lending her money. It's probably not a complete list. But I am sure that at some point, a boyfriend's compliance will make him look less attractive. Servility is not hot. You should put a ring on it first. Then as your husband he can serve you as he should—and he'll look more attractive for doing so.[26]

And for goodness sake, whether before or after marriage, don't belittle him to death. Your little conquests here will brutalize the mutual attraction you both desire, as he naturally grows demoralized and you naturally grow contemptuous.

### 7. Use food as the ally.

As with almost everything, the old wives were right here. One of the best ways to a man's heart is through his stomach. The reason, as I suggested above, is that the appetite for food is an ally to the appetite for sex.

As with men, there are two main ways to use food: the general and the focused. First, cultivate the general reputation as a provider of food. Be the woman who brings the food to the meeting, who likes to make and distribute baked goods, etc. If you're good at it, host dinner parties where you invite a large number of people—only a few of whom should be men you find attractive. Sometimes these men don't even need to be there: your reputation will spread to them indirectly.

Second, once you've reached a certain level of exclusivity with one man, give him food directly. Women and men both like food, but men associate it more with pleasant domesticity. And you want men to associate you with pleasant domesticity. Men want to be bound to a house—(be a *hus-band*)—only where it's nice and pleasant. And the prospect of food is very much a domestic pleasure.

Yes, it's that simple, crude, funny...and effective.

The very un-marriage-minded women and men may roll their eyes, or even ridicule you. Ignore them. They're not going where you're going.

Remember the words of the unexceptional woman with all the exceptional suitors: "I smile a lot. I laugh a lot. And I bake a lot." Be like her if you can. Do your best. Bend, don't break.

---

26  What is a duty in marriage is often a sin before marriage.

## 8. Be promiscuous with kindness.

The marriage-minded should focus on practicing general kindness, especially to the opposite sex. There are two main benefits to such kindness. First, you'll be more attractive. The opposite sex likes to observe your kindness. Almost everyone knows, at some level, that kindness is the chief virtue of the home. Spouses need it. And children really need it.

Second, by such kindness, you will be fostering a community where the sexes are less fearful, less suspicious, and more joyful with one another. Kindness in dating will thus produce less misogyny, less man-hating, and more friends to marriage, and thus more friends to your marriage. The woman that a man embitters today may be the friend, or the friend of a friend, of his future wife. The man a woman humiliates today may have a similar relationship with her future husband.

Instead, as you proceed with gentle persistence, be as kind as you can be. Remember that other people are as vulnerable as you are, some more so. Remember too that many people are deeply confused and often subject to painful alienation from the other sex and from themselves. Gentleman, don't speak about any woman's ugliness or sexual impropriety, even if it's true; place a veil over such things. Ladies, don't belittle or humiliate a man or men in general. It's not right, and it's not good for your future marriage. Men and women know where the jugular is, where the weak spot is: a woman's beauty and chastity, and a man's strength. Don't go for the jugular. Let's build each other up by mutual encouragement.

*How to Reject and Accept Rejection*

Rejection is a difficult and sensitive matter. Many painful rejections can be avoided by following the advice above: patiently guard the heart.

Nevertheless, deep but unrequited affection is always a danger—and it's very painful. When our beloved—whom we see in such glorious beauty—does not reciprocate our affections, we feel deeply un unlovable. We ascribe to them a vision equal to the strength of the beauty we see, so the rejection feels like a heavy judgment.

Still, the rejected person should try not to lash out in anger or sink into depression. Try instead to remember that although your beloved is wonderful to behold and you feel comparatively inferior and weak, the precise opposite is probably true as to vision. You probably have better vision than your beloved does.

Human beings have immense beauty, but our eyes often just don't see. You were given a gift: the ability to see something very, very good. The other party is probably just blind to your goodness and maybe also to his or her own. Don't get angry at them for their blindness.

The person doing the rejecting should remember the same. Avoid ignorant pity, but reflect with humility and gratitude that someone could see something so good in you—something that perhaps you can't even see in yourself.

It's the truth that sometimes rejection has to happen. If you don't see the possibility of all three unions with the admirer, including mutual bodily attraction, then you should say so with clarity, gratitude, and gentleness. Don't enumerate the reasons—you may not know them yourself. Don't enter negotiations. Instead, firmly and briefly, (1) compliment the other party in one or two ways, (2) express gratitude for the compliment of his or her affection, and (3) say that you don't think a mutually joyful marriage would be possible—and that it's nobody's fault.

The best rejections work that way. Over the years, I was blessed by more than one good rejection.

Rejection will be painful. And such a kind rejection may make you appear even more beautiful to the rejected—and thus increase his or her pain. But in the end, both of you will separate as better people, not bitter people, and more suited to marriage to the right person.

# CHAPTER SEVEN

## BUT WHY GET HITCHED?

*Peter Pan could never understand*
*Why Wendy darling wanted more than Neverland.*
*But a lost boy always makes it on his own,*
*So he never grew up, and he ended up alone.*

*But I would rather*
*Have you sittin' here next to me,*
*Tellin' bedtime stories*
*And singin' harmony.*[1]

The marriage-minded will often call into question their whole pursuit. They may have a persistent longing for marriage, but are less confident that the feeling makes any sense: "Sure I feel like entering this thing called marriage, but why should I obey this feeling? Is there any good *reason* why I should follow the *feeling*? After all, I may *feel* like quitting my job, eating a whole box of cookies, or going to a Star Trek convention dressed as an Imperial Stormtrooper. But such a feeling would not represent a sufficient *reason* for action. My feelings are sometimes stupid."

In this chapter, I aim to remind the reader of the non-stupid reasons

---

1    The Okee Dokee Brothers, *Along for the Ride* (2012). As someone wrote, it's just "not good that the man should be alone." Gen. 2:18.

for the feeling. The marriage-minded often need such a reminder, especially today.

When the marital reason coincides with the marital feeling, marriage makes much more sense. Further, the conviction that <u>marriage is good</u> makes the marital enterprise far more successful.

## A. Marriage made you

Most people feel like marriage. Their feeling has a good reason. The first and most important reason is that marriage made each of us. Human beings are, for the most part, *homemade*—children of marriage.

Let me explain. One of the things the modern university is nearly unanimous in affirming is that "marriage is a social construct." The assertion is closely related to the even more common assertion today that "gender is a social construct."

The alleged social "construction" of marriage and even gender is not a half truth and not even a quarter truth. It's nearly the precise opposite of the truth. Instead, both ancient common sense and modern science confirm that every individual (and thus society) is a male-female construct and, to a somewhat lesser extent, a marital construct.

Let's review facts rather than fiction.

### 1. *Male-and-female* made you

Every human being on this planet is a "gender construct" because he or she results from millions of male-female bonds. Here one finds the true, factual foundation of human solidarity and equality. Everyone, male and female, participates in this heritage, this tradition. We are equal.

Furthermore, in this equality there is a remarkable equality between the sexes. We now know by modern embryology, with its discovery of the mammalian egg and sperm, that in these bonds of gametes, each sex is equally necessary; each contributes essential genetic materials that make up a precisely equal part of each individual (23 chromosomes each). Furthermore, by affirming the antiquity of the human species, modern science has shown how many thousands of such bonds were absolutely necessary to make each one of us.

Further, of these male-female bonds, 99.9999% involved copulation. There may have been some very random non-copulatory transfer of gametes, but some measure of bodily intimacy probably was almost always involved. In other words, the union was not merely a union of gametes but a bodily union of male and female.

### 2. *Free male-and female* made you

We are children of freedom as well as equality. The vast majority of these copulations were free, not forcible. Common sense teaches this. With few exceptions, almost no one has the taste or tolerance for forcible sex. Almost all women find it horrific, almost all their parents have a similarly visceral reaction. Further, as to men, even on a raw appetitive level, the vast majority are strongly inclined to mutually pleasing sex. With so many people hating or at least disliking it, forcible sex was likely the exception rather than the rule.

Modern evolutionary science confirms that *freedom*, not *force*, made us. If millions of years of repeated forcible copulation had produced the modern woman, then she would not have such a visceral revulsion at the idea. Further, violence to the mother is very inhospitable to the health of the offspring—and thus to evolutionary survival. Children are much more likely to be conceived, to survive pregnancy, and to make it to fertile adulthood when their mother is not terrified of bodily violence by the father.

Besides evolutionary theory, modern anthropology further confirms the massive preponderance of freedom. We now know that nearly all of human generations occurred in millions of years before the Neolithic Revolution, which produced the agriculture and metallurgy that made human bondage and subjugation so much more possible and thus prevalent. Among primitive populations, relatively peaceful monogamy seems to have been the prevailing norm.[2]

---

2    For a recent review of this evidence, see William Tucker, *Marriage and Civilization: How Monogamy Made Us Human* (Washington, DC: Regenery Pub., 2014).

To be sure, extending over thousands of generations, we all will find in our family tree a violent copulation, perhaps several. Still, we are, in the main, sons and daughters of freedom—conceived in liberty.

### 3. *Marriage* made you.

Of the male-female bonds that made us, the vast majority involved not only *freedom* but some *marital bond*. By marital bond, I mean what the old common law called "marriage": the free agreement of a man and woman to engage in the joint enterprise, at once pleasant and laborious, of copulation and cohabitation, primarily for the reproduction and joint education of their offspring: no governmental license or public ceremony required.

The main reason we can conclude that our ancestry is largely marital is that marriage, so defined, made so much sense. Marriage represents an obvious convergent solution to a variety of perennial human challenges. Human beings, in the main, like freedom, company, conversation, and copulation, and we are strongly inclined to care for the offspring that often result from all that easy copulation—provided we know their identity.

These inclinations are very good for children because children are so desperately needy. With marital agreements, children are much, much more likely to exist, for copulation is a very efficient method of reproduction; and fertile copulation is far more likely to occur where cohabitation and conversation occur. Further, children are much, much more likely to survive when conceived in connection with a martial agreement, for their enormously intensive needs require that adults cohabit with them, converse with them, and otherwise care for them—and the most efficient way for children to enjoy these benefits is for their actual mother and the father to live together, converse together, and otherwise both stick around to help raise their common offspring.

Marriage, then, arises at the convergence of the intensive needs of children and the inclinations of adults. Common sense dictates that human beings would tend to arrive at this obvious solution. Our ancestors were almost certainly smart enough to figure this out—and we see marriage in virtually every culture.

One interesting issue, however, is whether the marital agreement preceded (and was "consummated") in the male-female bond. Very often the reproductive male-female bond may have occurred where the agreement was only prospective. That is, the male and female had sex but had not actually made any marital agreement. Still, the copulation had a pre-marital rather than non-marital character; that is to say, the parties understood at some level that if offspring did result from their bond, then a more lasting bond—the formation of a home—should follow suit. Such copulations, then, perhaps could be best described as proto-marital and not merely pre-marital. Stated otherwise, while sometimes the male-female bond consummated the marital agreement, frequently the marital agreement consummated the male-female bond. The "traditional" sequence of marriage-sex-baby was no doubt frequently replaced with sex-baby-marriage.

It would have seemed, however, that the solution more attentive to our nature, at once both rational and vulnerable, would be to insist that an express mutual agreement as to offspring precede the copulation. A culture requiring such agreements would give the woman greater assurance of male assistance in the joint education of offspring, in part by giving the man greater assurance as to the identity of his own offspring. Remember that the woman wants help, and the man wants to know that his own offspring will be the beneficiaries of his help. A pre-copulatory agreement provided greater assurance to both—and thus made more sense.

In sum: every human being on the planet is a result of countless male-female bonds. These bonds were almost all copulatory. Of these fertile bonds, almost all were free. Of these free fertile bonds, the vast majority were at least proto-marital, and most of these were probably marital.

Man is thus a male-female construct and (largely) a marital construct. In the main, we are equal. We are sons and daughters of liberty, not accident or force. We are sons and daughters of marriage, not fornication.

Therefore, the *feeling* toward marriage makes a lot of sense. Marriage made us—millions of years of marriage. Because we were made *by* marriage, we were made *for* marriage.

## B. If marriage made me, why is marriage so hard?

*People will not look forward to posterity, who never look backward to their ancestors.[3]*

If marriage is so natural to us, why does it seem so hard? I think the short answer is that sometimes Nature forgets and that, more often, Society forgets.

Nature forgets because she is not always reliable. Sometimes she fails to provide. Sometimes people lack the inclination to sex, or to the household, or to the care of their own offspring. Some people have all the inclinations but accident or circumstances prevent them from joining in the very tradition that made them. This whole topic involves philosophical and religious considerations that far exceed the subject of this little book. All I can say in candor is that, toward the marriage-minded, Nature seems wildly generous but sometimes forgetful.

Society forgets when it obscures or distorts the natural meaning and purpose of marriage. Society can, for instance, make impossible demands on marriage—for example, that marriage must be a place of perfectly fulfilling love, romantic bliss, or some other fantasy. Marriage can be fun and joyous, but such an earthly thing cannot secure celestial bliss.

Society forgets when people don't observe marriage around them. Children often don't see marriage; they can be conceived by force, by accident, by parents who never marry, who casually divorce, or who otherwise abandon the household. Such conception and such abandonment make it harder for the children to understand what marriage is and what it's good for. It can seem abstract or foreign.

Society forgets as men and women live increasingly alienated from one another. Men and women can view each other as aliens—with distrust,

---

3    Edmund Burke, *Reflections on the Revolution in France* (1790).

suspicion, and even hatred.

Society forgets when society as a whole goes from marriage's cheer-leader to marriage's boo-leader. Human beings like praise and dislike blame. Society can thus make marriage easier by praise or harder by sneer. After all, if marriage is irrelevant, or stupid, or oppressive—as has been frequently said—only a fool would pursue it.

In sum, for reasons of personal inexperience, personal distrust, social disinterest, and cultural hostility, marriage, although natural, can become obscure.

**C. We can overcome. Most everything you need to know about marriage you could have learned in kindergarten.**

> It won't be a stylish marriage.
> I can't afford a carriage.
> But you'll look sweet, on the seat
> Of a bicycle built for two.

So is there any way to recover some appreciation for "marriage"? For the marriage-minded, as they watch the decline in both the number and stability of marriages, marriage can seem increasingly foreign. The distance is acutely painful for those whose childhood home was not very marital. They watch *some* couples, even very old couples walk by, and, with longing, they wonder "how they met and what makes it last?"[4] Is it magic or dumb luck?

I think almost anyone can "get" marriage. You can understand how it can work, and more importantly, how you can make it work.

At the risk of oversimplification, let me say that most everything you need to know about marriage you could have learned in kindergarten. Most of the basic truths about marriage can be found in one song: "Daisy Bell" (a/k/a "Bicycle Built For Two"), written in 1892 by Harry Dacre. Now considered a *children's* song, it was once a general *popular* song when marriage was very popular.

---

4    Stephen Bishop, *It Might Be You* (1982).

The lyrics are chock-full of important lessons about marriage. Let's first review the well-known chorus.

**Refrain**

*Daisy, Daisy, give me your answer do.* Marriage begins with a free agreement, proposal and *answer*; it arises by reflection and choice, not accident or force. The very word spouse reflects this feature. It is a derivative from the Latin verb *spondere*, meaning to respond or answer.

*I'm half crazy all for the love of you.* Although rational and free, marriage is not all rational. Marriage engages not only the mind but also the heart and the body. Marriage should begin with a free mind, but half-craziness too—all the funny, problematic, joyous longings of the heart and body.

*It won't be a stylish marriage. / I can't afford a carriage.* In the West, the idea of marriage became infected with the dreams of other-worldly romance. The romance depicts the man sweeping the woman off her feet, with her being carried away to the cottage by the sea or even the castle in the sky. But marriage is terrestrial, not celestial, and it's about work and play, not lying around. The romantic ideal—the "stylish" stuff—has made a wreck of marriage, burdening it with expectations that no earthly thing can satisfy. The "stylish" marriage is not good for real marriage.

*But you'll look sweet upon the seat / of a bicycle built for two.* Rather than a stylish carriage ride, marriage is a ride on a bicycle built for two. This image is quite helpful in showing how marriage is both *attainable* and *sustainable*. It's more attainable to men because most can't afford the carriage—they can't offer a woman a life of leisure, but can hope to offer them a life of joint work and play (sometimes more work than play). It's more attainable to women because most aren't interested in lounging around—whether on top of a pedestal or on a chaise lounge. Women are human beings, and as such, they like to do something besides sitting—like work, play, enterprise of all sorts. In turn, marriage is thus more attractive to men. Most have rational and subrational preferences for women in motion instead of women at rest. Women "look sweet"

111

at work and play.

Marriage can seem more sustainable because the image explains what makes marriages work. Above all, marriage, like the bicycle-built-for-two, works because the partners work. They pedal. As in cycling, the work can be sometimes easy (flats), sometimes hard (uphill), sometimes unnecessary (downhill). Sometimes the downhills can be exhilarating.

Not all marriages follow the same course. Some have more uphills, some have more flats, some have crazy twists and turns. But almost no marriages have all easy downhills, requiring no work at all.

What does this work consist in? What are the pedals? Each spouse's two pedals consist in this simple twofold work: (1) try to please your spouse, and (2) try to be pleased with your spouse. Try to do what pleases your spouse, even if you have to bend a bit. And try to make a point of being pleased by your spouse—mainly by making a point of noticing their good qualities. Where both spouses are pedaling in this way, marriages are very strong, very enduring.

Lots of marriages, however, can do very well on just three pedals—where one of the parties fails to do the work of either pleasing or being pleased. Many marriages, I suspect, keep going with just two pedals—where, say, both parties are trying to please though forget to make a point of being pleased. Some marriages, though highly inequitable, slowly keep riding along even where one party alone works both pedals. Fewer marriages, I think, do well where only one pedal is worked—where, for instance, one spouse does nothing and the other relies solely on trying to please. But last and least are marriages where the couple, having enjoyed the downhill fun, reaches the flats, and concludes that the marriage has "failed" because further motion actually requires work. Instead of the premature defeatism, they should start pedaling, and keep pedaling. Usually, after some time, it's not that hard.

With this image in mind, I think almost any couple can make marriage work. If you're approaching marriage, ask yourself and your prospective spouse to make the following pledge:

(1) I will keep pedaling with both feet.

(2) If I fail to do that, I will pedal with one foot.

(3) If I fail to pedal at all, I will keep my feet on the pedals.

(4) If my feet slip, I will at least keep them off the ground.

(5) If my feet hit the ground, I will stay on the bike.

(6) If after all that, I fall or the bike falls, I will get back on the bike.

(7) And of course, I will not do anything so wrong and stupid as jumping off the bike and running away (e.g., to chase after another bike partner), and certainly never when vulnerable passengers (children) are on board.

Strengthen your resolve by making the promise in front of a bunch of people whose good opinion you cherish. Even better, make that promise before people who are friends to you, friends to marriage in general, and friends to your marriage. You want cheerleaders here. It makes marriage easier and more fun.

**First Verse**

Returning to the song, let's look at the first verse, which describes the singer's pre-proposal longing.

*There is a flower within my heart / Daisy, Daisy.* Marital longing is a matter of the heart as well as the head. And it is something beautiful, like a flower.

*Planted one day by a glancing dart / Planted by Daisy Bell.* Marital longing often begins with a glance or look. But that seed needs cultivation over time—hence it happened a while back—"one day." Don't propose marriage until some time has passed after the initial dart. Don't believe the romantic myth that you'll "know" immediately upon the first look.[5]

---

5    It is only with hindsight that a married man or woman can ascribe such significance to the look. You won't know anything until the look is supplemented by time and reflection.

*Whether she loves me or loves me not / Sometimes it's hard to tell.* Don't expect pre-marital certainty about mutual affection: Is she the one? Is his love pure? Is mine? You'll never get married if you're waiting for such *certainty*. Be prudent and thoughtful, but don't demand perfect clarity. There's always a leap of faith involved in any enterprise, whether commercial, marital, or otherwise.

*Yet I am longing to share the lot / Of beautiful Daisy Bell.* The longing to be desired is not to possess the other, but *to share his or her lot*—for better and for worse, in good times and in bad. That's the mutual longing the couple should aim for: a desire to share one life together.

**Second Verse**

The next verse treats the singer's vision of their future together.

*We will go 'tandem' as man and wife / Daisy, Daisy.* Yes, that's it.[6]

*Ped'ling away down the road of life / I and my Daisy Bell.* As I elaborated above, the marital work is like pedaling away down the road of life, with all its ups and downs. This work is sometimes irksome, sometimes a chore, sometimes fun, sometimes really fun.

*When the road's dark, we can both despise / Policemen and lamps as well.* Marriage arises in a community. Sometimes, when things get very bad in the household, the community's authority must intervene. But for the most part, from the beginning, the spouses should despise any such involvement. Rather, the couples should resolve to weather the tough times without resorting to the police, the courts—and still less the divorce courts.

*There are bright lights in the dazzling eyes / Of beautiful Daisy Bell.* Instead, the spouses should look to one another from the beginning—look to see if they have the goodness and wherewithal to be the partner to

---

6    For what it's worth, the use of "man and wife" is more egalitarian than "husband and wife." The word "wife," at origin simply means "woman" or female, so "man and wife" is closest to "male and female" or "man and woman." Husband and wife thus meant house-man and a woman. The closest parallel to *hus-band* would be "*hus-wife*"—still preserved, in a more specialized sense, as "housewife."

endure the tough times. Do you and your future spouse have that look of beautiful determination—eyes shining down the road of life? Daisy apparently had that look.

**Third Verse**

*I will stand by you in "wheel" or woe / Daisy, Daisy.* Marriage is serious, and marriage is playful. Therefore, the singer promises to stick with her, through thick or thin, but with a smile.

*You'll be the bell(e) which I'll ring you know / Sweet little Daisy Bell.* Marriage is playful, and marriage is about household affection. Of course he uses diminutives like "sweet" and "little." That's what people do in happy homes. Marriage is not about cold, arms-length respect. Marriage is about mutual affection that transcends mere formal respect.

*You'll take the lead in each trip we take / Then if I don't do well.* Marriage is not about equality but harmony. Every harmony requires a dominant note. Still the dominant note can change, and neither male nor female will always be in the lead. Further, the dominance is never asserted but permitted. In my husbandly opinion, I think the man should yield to the wife in most things, unless such yielding would be grossly imprudent or dishonorable.

*I will permit you to use the brake / My beautiful Daisy Bell!* The last verse ends with an exclamation—you are "mine" and you are "beautiful." The spouses do indeed possess one another, but not like one owns a car or pair of shoes. One's spouse is more like a trust, an endowment—to be cherished for life. And that mutual entrusting is truly something very, very beautiful.

For my part, I thank God for my beautiful wife. She is a great blessing to me. I hope to be a blessing to her.

Now go forth with prudence, confidence, and joy.

Made in the USA
Monee, IL
10 December 2020